EINSTEIN

VISIONARY SCIENTIST

$\mathcal{E}$INSTEIN

VISIONARY SCIENTIST

JOHN B. SEVERANCE

CLARION BOOKS ❧ NEW YORK

CLARION BOOKS
a Houghton Mifflin Company imprint
215 Park Avenue South, New York, NY 10003

Book design by Sylvia Frezzolini Severance.
Type is 12-point Sabon.

Printed in the U.S.A.

Library of Congress Cataloging-in-Publication Data

Severance, John B.
Einstein : visionary scientist / John B. Severance.
    p.   cm.
Includes bibliographical references and index.
    ISBN 0-395-93100-2
1. Einstein, Albert 1879–1955. 2. Physicists–Biography.
I. Title.
QC16.E5S394   1999
530'.092—dc21
[B]   98-51396
                         CIP

CRW 10 9 8 7 6 5 4 3 2 1

To my grandson,
David Severance Cushing,
who arrived upon the completion
of this manuscript

CONTENTS

Einstein explains an equation.

CHAPTER ONE

EINSTEIN'S
PLACE IN HISTORY

Imagine explaining to a group of six-year-olds that Alpha Centauri, the star closest to earth, is so far out in space that a voyage to it would take longer than their lifetimes. Most first graders think it will take them so long just to grow up that there will be plenty of time to go anywhere. A small dreamer might ask, "If we can land on the moon, how come we can't fly to the stars?" Albert Einstein said that because his early mental development was slow, he never thought of questions about the universe when he was little. Therefore, childish pre-conceptions did not confuse his later scientific thinking. "I began to wonder about space and time only when I had already grown up," he said. "Naturally, I could go deeper into the problem than a child." This, he explained, was how he came to develop the theory of relativity.

For the two hundred years before Einstein, physical science had been based on the theories of the Italian astronomer and mathematician Galileo Galilei (1564–1642) and the English philosopher and mathematician Sir Isaac Newton (1642–1727). There is a story that Galileo experimented by dropping objects from the Leaning Tower of Pisa. Whether or not this is true, he created controversy with his discovery that all falling bodies have the same velocity and the same rate of acceleration. He also constructed the first complete astronomical telescope. Supposedly, Newton began thinking about gravity when an apple fell on his head. Whatever got him started, he is best known for stating the laws of motion, including the law of gravitation that all particles and bodies in the universe are attracted to one another by the force of gravity. His most significant contribution to scientific technique was the development of calculus, an important branch of mathematics that is essential to modern science and technology.

Newton's theories were based on the idea that the universe worked somewhat like the cogwheels and springs inside a gigantic grandfather clock. By the end of the nineteenth century, a few physicists had begun to question this vision of a vast machine. In 1905, when Einstein was a twenty-six-year-old clerk in the Swiss patent office and did not yet have his Ph.D. in physics, he published four remarkable scientific papers. Denis Brian, in his book *Einstein: A Life,* writes, "His fourth paper . . . proved to be the most sensational, for it challenged Newton's view of the universe, one that had endured for two centuries." This was Einstein's special theory of relativity.

For the simplest introduction to the concept, imagine a bus moving down your street at ten miles per hour with a woman on board who is walking forward in the aisle to get off at the next stop. To the driver and all other seated people on the bus, the passenger is walking at three miles an hour. If you were looking out a window in your house, the woman would appear to be moving at her own speed plus

Galileo Galilei (1564–1642), Italian astronomer and mathematician, whose work was part of the foundation for Einstein's thinking.

Sir Isaac Newton (1642–1727), English philosopher and mathematician, whose laws of motion and theory of light were important to Einstein's work.

the speed of the bus, or thirteen miles per hour. But what if you magically changed your location and were now far out in the galaxy in a space station equipped with an extremely powerful telescope that had X-ray vision to see through the roof of the bus? Now, not only the woman and the bus would be moving but also the whole street and your house as well, along with the surface of the earth itself. A calculation of the speed of the woman has to include the rotation of the earth and the speed at which it is circling the sun, nineteen miles per second. The woman's speed is relative to where you are.

George Gamow, a physicist who wrote books on physics for non-physicists, said Einstein was the first to understand that the laws of nature work only within the limits of what we can see for ourselves. "For people of the ancient cultures," said Gamow, "the Earth was flat, but it certainly was not for Magellan, nor is it for the modern astronauts." On the foundations laid down by Isaac Newton, Albert Einstein began constructing the framework of modern physics and extended our knowledge of the universe.

Throughout his life, Einstein worked on refining his theories and developing new ones, but there were many other aspects of his career. Before World War I, he taught physics in universities at Prague, Zurich, and Berlin. Although he was born in Germany, he never loved his homeland. Because he was Jewish, he had to leave the anti-Semitic totalitarian state created by Adolf Hitler in the 1930s. Although he was not a religious Jew, Einstein became involved in the cause of Zionism, the movement that created the modern state of Israel. As his reputation grew, he was invited to lecture at many institutions in Europe, Asia, and the United States. Eventually, he took a position with the Institute for Advanced Study at Princeton University and, in 1940, became a U.S. citizen.

Many people mistakenly believe that Einstein was a member of the team that created the atomic bomb, but he was never directly involved. Some of his thinking, however, was the foundation for the laboratory experiments run by the scientists who figured out how to split an atom. This enabled other scientists to devise a way of releasing energy in the form of the colossal explosions that devastated two Japanese cities in 1945 and ended World War II.

Einstein was a pacifist, and he would no doubt prefer to be remembered for the more peaceful applications of his theories. Another of the four papers he published in 1905 discussed a theory of the behavior of light. His work in this field earned him the 1921 Nobel Prize in physics. The theory was fundamental to the invention of the phototube, a key element in the functioning of television and in the photoelectric cells that are used in burglar alarms, automatic

C. Francis Jenkins, who helped develop television, works the dial of an early set in 1930. Einstein's discovery of the law of photoelectric effect, for which he won the 1921 Nobel Prize, was fundamental to the invention of the phototube used in TV sets.

doors, and grocery-counting scanners in supermarkets. Einstein's work in photoelectrics also underlies the invention of the lasers that activate the compact disks we use to listen to music and that enable computers to store information. Lasers may soon be used to power spacecraft, thus reducing our dependence on fossil fuels.

Perhaps the early twentieth century was just the right moment in history for new thinking about space and time. In the art world of Paris in 1909, a new approach to painting was invented by Georges Braque and Pablo Picasso. Cubism, as it was called, was a rejection

Pablo Picasso, Spanish-born artist, in his Paris studio, 1920. Picasso was a dominant figure in the changing scene of twentieth-century art during the years when major changes were also taking place in science.

of the realistic representation of nature, which had been a main function of western art for centuries. One of the goals of cubist painting was to show several views of an object at the same time. For example, from your window you might see the profile of a car parked on your street. If you took the time to walk outside, stand at the front bumper, and open the hood to study the motor, you would have two more views of the car. In a cubist painting you would see the car's profile, the grille, and the motor all at the same time. Picasso and Einstein never worked together, but each did important creative work in the first few decades of the twentieth century, a time for new ideas in both art and science.

Albert Einstein with his sister, Maja, 1885.

CHAPTER TWO

A DIFFICULT START

In southern Germany on the Danube River, there is an ancient port called Ulm. Its greatest history took place in the Middle Ages, when its Gothic cathedral church, the second largest in Germany, was built. A block or two from the cathedral, in an apartment at 20 Bahnhofstrasse, Albert Einstein was born on March 14, 1879. His grandmother said he was much too heavy, and his mother thought the baby's head was too large and square. Hermann and Pauline Einstein became worried that their son might be mildly retarded. As he grew older, he seemed rather slow in learning to speak. There is a family story that his elementary school principal said it didn't matter what profession the boy prepared for because he would never be successful at anything.

In 1880, the Einsteins moved to nearby Munich, a city vibrating with commerce and culture, where Hermann set up an electrical equipment business with his brother Jakob. In November 1881,

Ulm, the German city where Einstein was born. His birthplace near the cathedral was bombed by Allied planes during World War II, but the cathedral itself was spared.

Albert's sister, Maria, called Maja, was born. Years later, she wrote an account of her brother's early childhood in which she included a description of his violent temper. He would throw things when annoyed, and she learned to run for cover as soon as his face went pale "and the tip of his nose snow white." Once, Albert just missed Maja with a bowling ball. Another time, when she didn't get away quickly enough, he whacked her on the head with the handle of a garden hoe. Fortunately, Albert's tantrums stopped at about the time he turned seven. In childhood, brother and sister established a deep love for each other that continued in adulthood until Maja died at the age of seventy.

Most of the time, Albert was a quiet child who seemed to have an inner life of his own. In old age, he explained that he did not talk much as a little boy because he wanted to speak in complete sentences. Therefore, before he could say anything, he had to put words and phrases together in his mind with deliberate care. Despite his later claim that questions about the universe did not occur to him as a child, Einstein seems to have begun the habit of scientific inquiry at an early age. He told a story about when he was sick in bed at the age of five and his father gave him a pocket compass to distract him from the misery of his illness. Many years later, Einstein wrote of his fasci-

A teacup portrait of Albert at about age six.

nation with the needle that "behaved in such a determined way," always pointing north no matter how he handled the compass. "I can still remember—or at least believe I can remember—that this experience made a deep and lasting impression on me. Something deeply hidden had to be behind things."

Albert was a solitary child who did not enjoy playing with other children. He especially did not like to play soldiers. One biographer, Philipp Frank, who knew Einstein personally, wrote, "When soldiers marched through the streets of Munich accompanied by the roll of drums and the shrill of fifes . . . little Albert . . . began to cry." Frank said that Einstein told his parents he had no desire to grow up to be "one of those poor people," a soldier. "He saw the parade as a movement of people compelled to be machines." Throughout his life, Einstein hated political tyranny or any situation where one group of people controlled the lives of others.

At an early age, Albert and Maja were introduced to literature and music by their parents. Many evenings Hermann Einstein read poetry to his family, often from the works of Johann Christoph Friedrich von Schiller and Heinrich Heine. Schiller celebrated human creativity and is regarded as a founder of modern German literature. Heine was influenced by the ideas of the French Revolution and is considered one of the greatest German lyric poets. Both poets were among Einstein's lifelong favorites. Pauline Einstein, who was an excellent pianist, wanted her children to appreciate music. Albert's first violin lesson at the age of six ended when he flung a chair at the teacher. His determined mother hired a new teacher, and the lessons continued until Albert was thirteen. For the rest of his life, Einstein often found diversion from the intensity of his scientific work by playing the violin.

In nineteenth-century Munich, children usually went to schools of their family's religion, but the Einsteins were not particularly religious Jews. The Jewish school was quite far away and the tuition fees were higher than at the nearby Catholic school. Also, the city's population was more than 80 percent Roman Catholic, so it is not surprising that Albert's first school was Catholic. Even though he was the only Jew in his class, he did not experience any discrimination. Because he was a dreamy student and spoke slowly, Albert did not do well in class, and his teachers considered him a bit stupid. The school was rather strict and the method of learning was entirely by rote. "The students were required to learn mechanically," wrote Philipp Frank, "and the main emphasis was placed on . . . obedience and discipline. The pupils were required to stand at attention when addressed by the teacher and were not supposed to speak unless asked a question." To Albert, this type of educational authority seemed identical to the military authority imposed on soldiers.

In some European countries, schools that prepare students for university study are called gymnasiums, and in 1888 Albert transferred to one called Luitpold Gymnasium. It was even more strict than the elementary school, but there was one teacher whom Albert liked because, unlike the other teachers, he did not require learning by rote. Herr Reuss, who taught the literature of Schiller, Johann Wolfgang von Goethe, and William Shakespeare, encouraged students to think for themselves. Albert did well in Latin because its grammar is logical, and he liked mathematics because it is a sort of scientific language. He got the highest marks in his class in these two subjects, but he refused to study anything that did not interest him. One irritated teacher remarked that he would prefer it if Albert were not in his class, to which the boy replied that he had done nothing wrong. "True," said the teacher, "but you sit there in the back row

Above: German poet and dramatist Friedrich von Schiller (1759–1805) was an important founder of modern German literature. His works were read to the family by Einstein's father, Hermann.

Above right: German romantic poet Heinrich Heine (1797–1856), another favorite of Hermann Einstein.

Right: Johann Wolfgang von Goethe (1749–1832), poet, dramatist, and novelist, whose work had a powerful and lasting effect on German literature.

and smile, and that violates the feeling of respect that a teacher needs from his class." Looking back on his school years in a speech he gave in New York, Einstein said, "The teachers in elementary school appeared to me like sergeants and in the gymnasium the teachers were like lieutenants."

At the elementary school, Albert had received Christian religious instruction. At the gymnasium, where students were required by law to study the faith of their families, he took instruction in Judaism. Although Albert's family was not religious, he developed a brief fascination with religion. He tried to persuade his family to eat only kosher food, and on his way to and from school, he sang hymns that he had composed in praise of God. Soon, however, he concluded that the authority of organized religion was as much of a tyranny as educational or military authority. He never lost his sense of spirituality, but for the rest of his life Einstein distrusted all forms of rigid authority. He preferred to withdraw into the private and individual life of scientific inquiry, where he could think for himself.

Nevertheless, Einstein's early religious training may have had an effect on his thinking. The Book of Genesis in the Old Testament says, "And God said let there be light: and there was light. And God saw the light, that it was good." The Gospel of Saint John in the New Testament says, "And the Word was God. . . . In him was life; and the life was the light of men. . . . That was the true Light which lighteth every man that cometh into the world." Light and enlightenment were to become very important aspects of Einstein's lifework.

Several people outside school had additional influences on Einstein's education, among them two uncles. His father's brother and partner in business, Uncle Jakob, was an electrical engineer who encouraged Albert's interest in mathematics. He often came to midday dinner with tricky algebra problems that Albert would solve while shouting in triumph. The other uncle was his mother's brother, Caesar Koch, a well-to-do grain merchant. Albert must have felt Uncle Caesar's respect and encouragement strongly, because years later he remembered him as "my best loved uncle." Even before the gymnasium days, Uncle Caesar had given the boy a model steam engine, which delighted him. A few years later, Albert sent his uncle a scientific paper describing an experiment he had thought up involving electricity and magnetism.

A street scene in Munich.

Another person who influenced Albert was a medical student named Max Talmey. It was the custom among European Jewish families to help impoverished students by regularly giving them good meals. Every Thursday, Talmey came to dinner at the Einstein house, and he and Albert became good friends even though there was a ten-year difference in their ages. In appreciation for the weekly meal, Talmey loaned Albert books on science, beginning with a series called Popular Books on Natural Science by Aaron Bernstein. Then he brought somewhat more advanced books such as *Force and Matter* by Ludwig Buchner and *Kosmos* by Alexander von Humboldt. The book that made the greatest impression was a geometry textbook that Talmey loaned to twelve-year-old Albert. "After a short while . . . he had worked through the whole book," wrote Talmey years later. "He thereupon devoted himself to higher mathematics, studying all by

Albert Einstein at age thirteen.

himself. . . . Soon the flight of his mathematical genius was so high that I could no longer follow." Talmey then recommended various books on philosophy, including *A Critique of Pure Reason* by Immanuel Kant. This book is often difficult for students in graduate school but it was apparently no problem for Albert. "At that time he was . . . only thirteen years old," Talmey wrote, "yet Kant's works, incomprehensible to ordinary mortals, seemed clear to him."

When Albert was fifteen, there was a sudden change in the life of the Einstein family. The electrical equipment business had been faltering, and the two brothers, Hermann and Jakob, decided they might do better in Italy. In June 1894, the house was sold and the family moved to Milan, leaving Albert to live in a boarding house in Munich while earning his diploma at the gymnasium. He needed the diploma if he wanted to go to a university, but he had never been happy submitting himself to the authority of the gymnasium. Furthermore, if he remained in Germany until he turned sixteen, he would be required by law to submit to the additional authority of national military service. He became depressed and explained his dismal situation to the family doctor, who wrote a certificate stating that Albert's condition could lead to a nervous breakdown. With this paper plus one from his math teacher explaining that Albert had gone beyond what the Luitpold Gymnasium could teach him in mathematics, he hoped to withdraw from school. The Luitpold administration had already decided that the school would be better off without him, and six months after the Einsteins moved to Milan, Albert joined them as a high-school dropout.

Albert loved the warmth of the Italian people, their art galleries, and their music. Maja said she had never seen him so cheerful and outgoing. With new friends, he hiked in the Apennine Mountains, the

Street scene in Milan.

first time in his life he had enjoyed physical activity. For the moment, this happy life was just what Albert needed, but it could not last. His father pointed out that it was necessary to face some practical matters. He had to finish his education or he had to go to work. He could not play forever.

Without his gymnasium diploma, Albert could not go to a university, but there was a technical school in Switzerland he could attend if he passed the entrance exams. In the spring of 1895 he took the exams for the Swiss Federal Institute of Technology in Zurich. At that time, the Swiss name for the institute was Eidgenossische

Hermann Einstein, Albert's father.

Technische Hochschule, or ETH, for short. Albert did brilliantly in mathematics but flunked biology, chemistry, and French. The head of the school was so impressed with his outstanding ability in math that he offered to accept Albert the following year without the exams if he could get a high-school diploma. For the next year, Albert went to a high school in the Swiss town of Aarau, close to the German border. He lived with the family of one of the teachers, Jost Winteler, and the open and encouraging educational atmosphere at school caused Albert's mind to blossom. He began to teach himself calculus, and it was then that he first wondered what the universe would look like if he could hitch a ride on a beam of light.

The seven Winteler children treated Albert as one of them. The whole family reveled in weekend outings in the clear mountain air, and soon Albert and the oldest daughter, eighteen-year-old Marie, found themselves in love. At home in the cheerful Winteler house, they often played lively piano and violin duets, and during vacations, they exchanged fervent letters. Biographer Denis Brian quotes a letter Marie received from Italy in which Albert describes her as "my dear little sunshine" and closes with "You mean more to my soul than the whole world did before."

The following year, when Albert was at ETH in Zurich and Marie was teaching first grade in another town, the letters continued. Then Albert stopped writing. He was unable to tell Marie that he had found a new love, Mileva Maric, a quiet young woman in his physics class. In fact, she was the only woman at the school, as it was rare in those days for women to seek higher education, especially in science. Most of his friends were puzzled by the relationship because Mileva was rather moody, had a slight limp due to a defective hip, and was three and a half years older than Albert. The only explanation seemed to be that they offered each other mutual support in the midst of an all-Swiss student body. Mileva was from Serbia, and Albert was stateless because he had renounced his German citizenship when he moved to Italy. He had applied for Swiss citizenship but would not receive it until 1901. Einstein later wrote that from age fifteen to twenty-one he was "entirely without state papers."

In Zurich, Albert and Mileva had a pleasant social life with classmates Marcel Grossman and Michele Angelo Besso, going to concerts and theaters as well as to parties, where Albert sometimes played his violin. On the lake in Zurich, Albert took up sailing, which became a lifelong diversion. It might not have mattered much what he wore

Einstein as a student in Zurich.

while sailing, even when Mileva was aboard, but his attitude to clothing was always unconventional. The mother of one of his school friends once asked Albert what on earth he was wearing around his neck. He explained that when hurrying out of his boarding house that morning, he had hastily snatched the runner off the piano to use as a scarf.

Zurich in the early twentieth century.

Albert also found plenty of time to study at ETH, but he worked only on projects that interested him. He was heading for a career as a teacher of mathematical physics, so his courses naturally included advanced geometry and calculus as well as astrophysics and astronomy. He also took courses in literature and philosophy. Einstein had great respect for his math teacher, Hermann Minkowski, even though the professor thought Albert was lazy. On the other hand, he found his physics teacher, Heinrich Friedrich Weber, rigidly conservative. In teaching physics, Weber chose to ignore the work of modern scientists, who were then questioning some of the principles of the classical physics of the past two centuries. In an effort to understand the newer physicists, Albert invented his own laboratory experiments, but according to Philipp Frank, his teacher disapproved. "You are a smart boy, Einstein," said Professor Weber, "a very smart boy. But you have one great fault: you do not let yourself be told anything."

On July 28, 1900, Einstein received his diploma from the board of examiners at ETH. He had scored well on the final exams, but Mileva had failed. Albert consoled her and urged her to try again the following year. She agreed, and the two began to think about getting married. When Maja learned of the plan, she advised Albert to keep it secret from their mother, who was already strongly opposed to the relationship, but he told her anyway. "Mama threw herself on her bed," wrote Albert in a letter to Mileva, "buried her head in the pillows and wept like a child." She told him he was ruining his future, and the next day she complained that by the time Albert was thirty Mileva would be "an old witch." Hermann Einstein had another reason for opposing the wedding. He pointed out that Pauline's relatives, who had paid Albert's tuition at the polytechnic, were no longer supporting him, and he was on his own financially. With no job in sight, he had no business considering marriage.

Finding a job was, in fact, a difficult project. Albert was the only one in his graduating class who was not offered an appointment as assistant professor at ETH. In his four years as a student he had managed to make enemies of many of his teachers. Professor Minkowski thought he was a "lazy dog," and Professor Weber thought he was arrogant. His only friend on the staff was a professor of history, who could not help much with an appointment in physics. As a recently naturalized Swiss citizen, Albert would not have the same chance for a job as applicants who were born Swiss. Therefore, he sent applications for teaching positions all over Germany and also in Italy, but none of these resulted in a job.

Pauline Einstein,
Albert's mother.

Meanwhile, his friend Marcel Grossman had arranged to have Albert recommended to the director of the Swiss patent office in Bern. It would, however, be a long time before Albert would know what job, if any, was available and if he had been accepted. Then, unexpectedly, he had an offer for a temporary position at a school in the town of Winterthur, filling in for a teacher who had to do his national military service from May to July 1901. Albert accepted the job, found lodging in Winterthur, and on Sundays returned to Zurich by train to visit Mileva.

In a letter to Mileva following one of these visits, Albert wrote about how delighted he had been "to press your dear little person to me in the way nature created it." When it turned out that Mileva had become pregnant, Albert's response was remarkably casual. "My dear kitten," he wrote, "I have just read a wonderful paper . . . on the generation of cathode rays by ultraviolet light. Under the influence of this piece I am filled with such happiness and joy that I absolutely must share it with you." Then after some vague reassurances about the future, he wrote, "How are you, darling? How's the boy? Can you imagine how pleasant it will be when we are able to work again?" Albert could not have known the baby's sex. Nevertheless, he blithely assumed it would be a boy, and his preoccupation with physics seemed to prevent any serious thought of how its arrival would change their lives. Later in the summer, Mileva learned that once again she had failed her exams at ETH. Albert told her not to worry, as they could still be a team in physics research. He did not think to ask if that was what she wanted to do with her life.

Switzerland at this time was a very conservative country, and illegitimate births were frowned upon, especially if the father was unemployed. If Albert had any hope of eventually getting a government job at the patent office, it was not a good time for him to marry a woman who was already carrying his child. His Swiss citizenship, granted earlier in the year, could be revoked. Furthermore, Pauline and Hermann's vehement opposition to the marriage would be even more strenuous if they learned they were soon to become grandparents.

Mileva's parents had not been informed, either. In the fall of 1901, it was a relief for Albert to land a tutoring job at a school in

Schaffhausen. The salary was extremely small, and he could barely afford occasional trips to see Mileva, thirty miles away in Zurich. Between visits they wrote frequently to each other. By now they were hoping the child might be a girl, whom they would name Liserl. After four months and several confrontations about his relaxed style of teaching, Albert was fired. He moved to Bern, took a gloomy little apartment, and advertised lessons in mathematics and physics.

Mileva went to her parents' home in Novi Sad, Serbia, to have her baby. A letter from her father on February 4, 1902, informed Einstein that Liserl had been born, but Mileva was too worn out to write. Albert replied immediately, asking the color of the baby's eyes and whom she resembled. Was she bald, and could he have a picture? He said he loved her already even though he had not yet seen her. Probably he never did see her. She may have been adopted by Mileva's relatives and possibly she contracted scarlet fever, which in those days often killed infants, but there is no record of what became of her.

Earlier, in Milan, Hermann Einstein's shaky business had gone bankrupt, and he had asked Albert to help pay for Maja's education. Albert was unable to make a significant contribution. But even with personal and financial problems hanging over his head, he could not be diverted from intellectual activities. The first student to appear at his door in response to the ad for math and physics lessons was a poor Hungarian named Maurice Solovine. He was more interested in philosophy than in physics or math. During the next two hours of animated philosophical conversation, Einstein and Solovine began a lifelong friendship, and in future discussions they were joined by one of Einstein's friends, Conrad Habicht. The meetings were accompanied by modest meals of sausages, cheese, hard-boiled

*Street in Bern,
the Swiss city
where Einstein's
life would
change.*

eggs, fruit, and cups of tea or Turkish coffee, and sometimes got so
raucous that the neighbors complained. The group, calling itself the
Olympia Academy, continued for years, with new members joining
and others leaving. The discussions had a strong influence on
Einstein's work, but for the time being, driven closer to starvation,
he was forced to move to an even cheaper apartment in the spring
of 1902.

On June 16, 1902, Albert received the exciting news that a week later he was to begin work at the patent office as a technical expert third class. Two years before he would have scorned such a nonacademic job, but now it meant survival. It was also a major turning point in Einstein's life.

Einstein at the time he was working in the Swiss Patent Office.

CHAPTER THREE

BUILDING A CAREER

In early October 1902, Einstein's father had a serious heart attack, and Albert traveled to Milan in time to be with him before he died. He took his father's death very hard perhaps because, on his deathbed, Hermann finally consented to the marriage of Mileva and Albert. The two were married in Bern on January 6, 1903, and they immediately settled down to a quiet domestic life. In the autumn, while on a trip to see her family, Mileva wrote to Albert that she had discovered she was again pregnant. He wrote back that he was happy she was "hatching a new chick," but he thought she had been gone long enough. "A good little wife shouldn't leave her husband alone," he wrote. "Things don't look nearly so bad at home as you think. You will be able to clean up in short order."

The year 1904 was a good one for the Einsteins. In May, Mileva gave birth to their son Hans Albert, and in September, Albert received a small raise in his salary at the patent office. Years later, Einstein said that Mileva had lost her interest in science by the time they were married. Twice failing her exams and having a baby before she was married may have slowed her down. Nevertheless, she sat in on meetings of the Olympia Academy and helped a great deal with her husband's work by looking up information and checking his math.

Albert's own interest in physics was now extremely intense. This may appear odd because he was isolated from the world of science. He had no doctorate, no laboratory, and almost no contact with other scientists, but professional isolation may have been just what he needed at the time. Much later, he would occasionally remark that his years in Bern were the happiest of his life. His brain was simmering with startling new ideas about physics, which he described in letters to his former schoolmate Michele Besso, now living in Trieste. In 1904, Besso took a job at the Swiss patent office that Einstein had urged him to apply for so the two could converse face to face. They would walk to and from the office while Einstein tried out fresh ideas on Besso. "I could not have found a better sounding board in the whole of Europe," Einstein said later.

The breathless work came together almost miraculously through-out 1905, in the course of which Einstein published four related papers in the prestigious German scientific journal *Annalen der Physik* (Annals of Physics). One of them earned him his Ph.D., and another, on the photoelectric effect, led eventually to the 1921 Nobel Prize in physics. A third one, on mass and energy, laid the groundwork that later led other scientists to the development of nuclear fission and the atomic bomb. But the paper that would change our understanding of the universe was "On the Electrodynamics of Moving Bodies," better known as the special theory of relativity.

All of these theories are very complex. Thousands of books and essays have been written to explain them for scientists as well as non-scientists. To condense the theory of relativity into a few paragraphs would be an extremely formidable task in this discussion of Einstein's life. It is possible, however, to develop an understanding of what the concept is about.

In his six-hundred-page biography of Einstein, Ronald Clark states that if Einstein's special theory of relativity can be reduced to a single sentence it would be, "One man's 'now' is another man's 'then.'" This simple statement may seem like nonsense to people who have not studied physics and higher mathematics. Many of Einstein's ideas appear to ignore common sense. After ten years of thinking about light and its speed, he had developed a theory of things that seemed to contradict what we can observe in everyday situations. For example, Einstein predicted that it would be possible to prove that gravity affects time. Contrary to common sense, clocks would be shown to run slower at high speeds. Many years after Einstein died, the National Aeronautics and Space Administration (NASA) conducted an experiment with a highly accurate atomic clock aboard a rocket. The results showed that Einstein's calculations had been correct.

The special theory also stated that moving objects contract as they accelerate. This suggested a need for a fresh look at the dimensions of things and the space they occupy as well as the relative behavior of time. In an effort to clarify the significance of Einstein's view of space and time, Ronald Clark asks three questions: What are "real" space and "real" time? How come no one ever before had thought what Einstein thought? What difference can Einstein's observations make to most people, or to put it more simply, who cares?

The answer to the first question is that real space and real time are whatever is real for the observer. "Just as beauty lies in the eye of the beholder," says Clark, "so does each man carry with him his own space and his own time." It depends on where you are.

To help answer the second question, Clark quotes British philosopher Bertrand Russell. "Nature . . . had educated common sense only up to the level of everyday life." We do not easily observe things traveling at, say, half the speed of light, 93,000 miles per second. With objects moving at much slower speeds, we cannot see the effects Einstein predicted. It is impossible to measure the infinitesimally slight shrinkage of a Frisbee whizzing across the back yard or even a jet plane leaving its vapor trail high overhead. The clock on the dashboard of a car that has been driven all day at fifty-five miles an hour does not show a different time from the clock on the kitchen wall.

The third question explores the relationship between physics and the rest of the world. If, as Clark says, "the special theory of relativity appears to deal with matters that are outside the range of human experience," why should anyone other than physicists care about Einstein's work? The simple answer is that Einstein's theory was timely. He wrote his thirty-page essay just when scientists were considering new extremes. As science moved from the nineteenth century into the twentieth, particles smaller than atoms were being discovered that could move at speeds fairly close to the speed of light. At the same time, astronomers were seeking new knowledge of space beyond our own galaxy. It was important to learn that Newton's mechanical concepts of space and time were actually related variables. When considered relative to speeds far beyond human experience, such as speeds approaching the speed of light, 186,000 miles per second, space and time had to be thought of together as space-time. The special theory of relativity showed that, despite centuries of theorizing, science was able to explain only a small segment of the vast complexity of the universe. There is much more to it than scientists had thought.

The genius of Einstein lay in the fact that just when the world of science needed new explanations, he was able to imagine possibilities beyond the mechanical world of Isaac Newton. But he never claimed that his work was totally original. Some years later, when he had become famous, Einstein noted in a speech that Galileo, Newton, and the Dutch physicist Hendrick Lorentz had "laid the foundations of physics on which I have been able to construct my theory."

At first, Einstein was disappointed that there was no immediate reaction to his 1905 publications. The spectacular theoretical work, done entirely in his head, still needed to be backed up with laboratory experiments and mathematical proofs. In less than a decade, however,

Dutch physicist Hendrick Lorentz, whose work influenced Einstein, later became his friend and mentor.

he was propelled into a community of the leading scientists of Europe. The first stirring of interest appeared early in 1906 in a letter from the prominent German physicist Max Planck asking questions about relativity. In his biography of Einstein, Denis Brian explains that Planck, who had also been investigating problems of light and energy, had come up with a theory of his own. "His new disturbing theory," writes Brian, "showed that instead of flowing in a steady uninterrupted stream, light, heat, and other forms of radiation moved in separate pieces of energy, which he called 'quanta.' . . . Many previous ideas about matter, energy and cause-and-effect were bound to be false." Although he was never certain about Planck's theory and its later developments, Einstein conducted a lifelong search for a connection between Planck's quantum physics and his own theories of relativity.

German physicist Max Planck was the first European scientist to ask Einstein about his theory of relativity.

The first academic job offered to Einstein was a position as a *privatdozent,* or apprentice lecturer, at the University of Bern. In European university systems at the time, this was the required first step toward becoming a professor. Because the work was unsalaried, Einstein had to keep his job at the patent office.

The next great boost came from Hermann Minkowski, his former mathematics teacher at ETH. In a paper published in 1907 and in a lecture in 1908, Minkowski demonstrated a mathematical interpretation of the special theory of relativity by means of geometry. For scientists and mathematicians, this was a simple way to understand the new and complex theory. The professor must have decided that his former student was no longer a lazy dog, but the two never had a chance to work together, for Minkowski died suddenly in January 1909.

Earlier, Einstein had been recommended for a newly created position as associate professor and head of theoretical physics at the University of Zurich, but the appointment had become bogged down in politics. Another candidate was a friend of Einstein's named Friedrich Adler, son of the founder of the Austrian Social Democratic Party. Most of the officials who were to agree on the appointment were Swiss Social Democrats and so the position went to Adler even though Einstein was the better choice. When Adler learned that his father's name had won him the job, he refused it. "If it is possible to obtain a man like Einstein for our university," wrote Adler, "it would be absurd to appoint me. I must quite frankly say that my ability as a research physicist does not bear even the slightest comparison to Einstein's." On July 6, 1909, Einstein resigned from the patent office and moved on to his first salaried academic position.

Einstein nearly missed his next step toward recognition in the European scientific community when he threw away what he thought was a piece of junk mail. Fortunately, the administration of the University of Geneva sent a second letter asking if he would accept an honorary doctorate. The institution was celebrating its 350th anniversary, and a number of well-known European scientists were being given honorary degrees. Among these were the wealthy industrial chemist Ernest Solvay, from Belgium, and the Polish-born scientist Marie Sklodowska Curie, from France. Curie was famous for her discovery of radium. For research in radioactivity, she, her husband, Pierre, and Henri Becquerel had been the joint recipients of the 1903 Nobel Prize in physics.

Later that summer, Einstein was invited to give a talk at a conference of leading scientists, including Max Planck, in Salzburg, Austria. One of Planck's students, a young woman named Lise Meitner, was present, and years later, she recalled that she did not at the time fully understand the "revolutionary transformation of our concepts of time and space," but she was impressed. She wrote that from his theory of relativity Einstein derived "the equation: energy=mass times the square of the velocity of light." This was the now famous formula $E=mc^2$. Lise Meitner found the information "overwhelmingly new and surprising." The thirty-year-old Einstein was well on his way to becoming a leading scientist himself.

Mileva, Albert, and their son, Hans Albert, moved to Zurich in October 1909. It was a new sort of life for the family. For Einstein himself, it was more time consuming than the patent-office job in Bern. He had only six to eight hours of actual classroom time per week, but to prepare the lectures and seminars as thoroughly as he thought he should took a great many more hours than he had expected. He had less time for original research. Furthermore, he became quite popular with his students. Often discussions of physics were continued after

Polish-born French scientist Marie Curie, discoverer of radium, in her Paris laboratory.

class in the cafés of Zurich, and sometimes Albert would bring a group of students home without telling his wife in advance. Mileva already had to put up with other students whom the Einsteins took in as boarders in order to supplement Albert's salary. The family finances were stressed by the formal dinner parties that the university expected

Above: Salzburg, where Einstein gave one of the lectures that helped make him famous.

Left: Prague, where Einstein held his first job outside Switzerland.

professors and their wives to host from time to time. On July 28, 1910, the birth of the Einsteins' second son, Eduard, caused additional demands on time and money.

This situation was not to last long. Einstein had hardly finished his first term in Zurich when he was approached about the possibility of accepting a position at the German University of Prague. Today the capital of the Czech Republic, Prague then belonged to the Austrian Empire. After some political complications about whether or not a German-born Swiss citizen should be allowed to take a job in a German institution located in an Austrian city, the post was given to Einstein. As a full professor, he was earning a higher salary than he ever had before, and his professional reputation was greatly enhanced, but there were risks.

Living in Prague could be difficult for a German Jew. More than half the Germans in Prague were Jewish. The Czech citizens of Prague assumed that all Jews were spies for Germany, and the non-Jewish Germans in Prague were developing a hatred for Jews that would reach its peak in the Holocaust during World War II. As a teenager, Einstein had come to distrust all organized religion, but he could not ignore it now. The elderly Emperor Franz Josef of Austria had decided that university positions in his empire should go only to people who were members of a recognized religion. In the blank for religion on the official job form, Einstein wrote "Mosaisch," the Austrian word for Jewish. Although he regarded the ethnic divisions of Prague as unimportant, Einstein drifted into the Jewish community. This included a number of philosophers and writers who were attracted to Zionism, a movement that worked toward the founding of the Jewish state now called Israel. Einstein was not persuaded to become a Zionist, but for the first time in his life, he had to face the problems of Jews in Europe.

Albert Einstein in about 1920.

CHAPTER FOUR

BECOMING FAMOUS

A lbert Einstein was a dreamer. Professors meeting their new colleague for the first time were drawn to his cheerful good humor and warm laughter, but most of them misunderstood the relaxed look in his large dark eyes. It was the look of a man who was not really focused on his immediate surroundings, whose mind was deeply preoccupied with questions few people could imagine and even fewer could answer. Some people who got to know him better thought that he lacked emotion and cared little for fellow humans. Others saw him as a scientific genius whose energies were devoted entirely to developing new and remarkable theories in the world of physics. It was, in fact, his work on photoelectric effects that in 1911 got him invited to read a paper at the first Solvay Congress in Brussels, Belgium.

The conference had been suggested by chemist Walther Nernst of Berlin, who would be the recipient of the 1920 Nobel Prize in chemistry. It was a meeting of twenty of the most outstanding European scientists and was organized by Einstein's acquaintance Ernest Solvay of Belgium. Another friend, Madame Curie, was one of the scientists from France. As the 1911 recipient of the Nobel Prize in physics, Curie became the first person to be awarded two Nobel Prizes. Another participant, Ernest Rutherford from England, had been awarded the 1908 Nobel Prize in chemistry for his research in radioactivity. Max Planck from Germany would receive the Nobel Prize for his quantum theory in 1918. The Dutch physicist Hendrick Lorentz, corecipient of the 1902 Nobel Prize in physics, presided over the meeting.

Ernest Rutherford.

Nernst brought along one of his students, Frederick Lindemann, who was born in Germany to an American mother. Later, Lindemann studied in Paris, became a professor at Oxford University in England, and was one of Winston Churchill's closest friends as well as his science adviser during World War II. The Solvay Congress was a rare moment of international sharing of scientific knowledge, and Einstein had a remarkable effect on the other scientists present. In a letter to his father, Lindemann wrote, "I got on very well with Einstein, who made the most impression on me except perhaps Lorentz." Madame Curie wrote later that she had "appreciated the clearness of his mind . . . and the depth of his knowledge."

The name of the young physicist was becoming well known in the science community of Europe and even in America. Many universities wanted him on their faculties. Even before the Solvay Congress, serious efforts had been made to persuade him to accept a position at the University of Utrecht in Holland. At the conference, Lorentz may have renewed the offer, and there were opportunities in Vienna and at Columbia University in New York. Ultimately, Einstein was persuaded to return to ETH in Zurich by his old friend Marcel Grossman, who had become dean of the math and science division.

As far as Mileva was concerned, this should have been an excellent move. Although they were financially better off in Prague, she was not at all happy there and longed for Zurich, where, perhaps, she had felt closer to her husband. Possibly, she was frustrated by Albert's growing reputation while she, with scientific training similar to his, was left to look after "the little bears," as the Einstein boys were called. She might also have suffered continuing depression over the loss of Liserl. Whatever the reasons, Mileva and Albert were drifting apart as he became more intensely occupied with his research. Their

Mileva and Albert's two sons with their mother. Eduard is on the left, Hans Albert on the right.

relationship was not improved by the continuing multitude of professional opportunities.

Even before the Einstein family returned to Zurich in the summer of 1912, Albert made a trip to Berlin to discuss the details of a research job he had been offered. During his stay, he visited a cousin five years older than he, whom he had not seen since childhood. Elsa Lowenthal was recently divorced and now lived in Berlin with her two teenage daughters, Ilse and Margot. Einstein already had a ten-year contract with ETH, and the idea of returning to Germany and the rigid culture that he had come to hate while growing up was not attractive. He declined the job offer but continued the new contact with Elsa by mail. She sent her letters to Einstein's office at the polytechnic because he had warned her that Mileva was a very jealous woman.

Einstein now began to work feverishly on a theory of gravitation. He found the project so difficult that he asked Marcel Grossman to help him with the math, and he often interrupted his work to deliver lectures at other institutions. These were also difficult and so abstract that many scientists could not understand them. One graduate student recalled a lecture Einstein gave at the University of Göttingen, Germany. "Here was this man talking . . . about space-time," he wrote, "and showing how you could explain gravitation by the way a body moves in space-time. . . . This was all so abstract that it became unreal to them. I remember seeing one of the professors getting up and walking out in a rage."

Another lecture was in Paris, to the French Society of Physicists in March 1913. Albert took Mileva with him on this trip, and they stayed with Marie Curie. They were so delighted with her hospitality in showing them the French capital that they invited Curie to bring two of her daughters to Switzerland for a hiking holiday with them and their boys. Once on that summer vacation, Marie challenged Albert to name all the mountain peaks they could see. Most of the time, however, the two scientists ignored the magnificent alpine scenery around them and the delicate edelweiss flowers at their feet while they talked about physics. During one discussion, Einstein grabbed Curie's arm and said, "What I need to know is exactly what happens to the passengers in an elevator when it falls into emptiness." He assumed that they would float, not feeling their own weight, but he wanted to explain the phenomenon in mathematical terms as a problem in relativity.

In a letter to Elsa, Einstein wrote, "Madame Curie is very intelligent but as cold as a herring," and speaking of the hiking trip some years later, he remarked that "Madame Curie never heard the birds sing." In spite of these ungracious comments, he had a high regard for her scientific abilities and described Curie as a "brilliant exception" to his belief that most women were incapable of truly outstanding achievements in science. This was not an unusual belief for the times, and Einstein was actually ahead of his time in thinking that women at least deserved equal opportunity to work in science.

In the spring of 1913, his friends Walther Nernst and Max Planck arrived in Zurich, hoping to persuade Einstein to accept a package deal. He would be a professor at the University of Berlin, the director of a new physics institute to be called the Kaiser Wilhelm Gesellschaft, and a member of the prestigious Prussian Academy of Sciences. This new opportunity to return to the native country he had been so anxious to leave when he was fifteen was no more appealing to Einstein now than it had been the summer before. The professional rewards, however, were hard to refuse, and he would be in the company of some the greatest physicists in Europe.

Without consulting his wife, he accepted the offer. He overlooked the fact that Mileva did not get along with his mother, Pauline, who had recently gone to live with her brother and sister-in-law in Berlin. When Albert told Mileva of his decision, she was extremely upset. "My wife howls unceasingly about Berlin and her fear of my relatives," wrote Einstein in a letter to Elsa. "Well, there is some truth in it. My mother is of a good disposition but . . . a true devil as mother-in-law. When she is with us, then everything is filled with dynamite."

Berlin traffic about 1913.

Despite the domestic tensions, the Einstein family moved to Berlin in the spring of 1914. By midsummer, Mileva had taken the boys back to Zurich because she hated Berlin and could not get along with Albert's mother. In August, political tensions that had been brewing among Austria, Serbia, Germany, Russia, France, and England finally erupted in the Great War, later called World War I. Einstein shipped the family furniture back to Switzerland but refused to give up his work in Berlin. He promised to send Mileva quarterly payments for household expenses.

Even before it became clear how horrible the first major war of the twentieth century would be, Einstein was opposed to the war on moral grounds. In October 1914, a document appeared called the "Manifesto of the 93." Ninety-three scientific and intellectual leaders in

Germany had signed this manifesto, which supported German militarism and its actions. A biologist at the University of Berlin asked Einstein to sign a "Manifesto for Europeans" in opposition to the war. It stated, "Never before has any war so completely disrupted cultural cooperation. It has done so at the very time when progress in technology and communications clearly suggest . . . the need for . . . a universal worldwide civilization. . . . The first step in this direction would be . . . to organize a League of Europeans." In addition to Einstein, only three other professors signed the document. A great many of Einstein's colleagues would have accused him of being a traitor if he had not been a Swiss citizen.

Australian and New Zealand ANZACs at Gallipoli, Turkey, one of the more disastrous campaigns of World War I.

A shell torn village in France.

Einstein, in his turn, regarded most of his colleagues as crazed by the fever of nationalism. He was especially upset with his friend Nernst for helping to develop chemical warfare. One result of the work was mustard gas, a deadly poison that eventually killed hundreds of thousands of people during the war and left thousands of survivors with seared lungs that caused them painful wheezing for the rest of their lives.

In the fall of 1915, Einstein put his indignation, his pacifism, and his personal life on hold to devote all his energy to the conclusion of his work on gravitation and the nature of the universe. He had been developing calculations for the project since his days in Prague, and he now worked day and night, skipping sleep and meals and leaving most of his mail unanswered.

A good background in mathematics and physics is needed to completely understand Einstein's concept of space-time. For a simple notion of the universe as Einstein was seeing it, we must put aside the idea of gravity as a force pulling between bodies. Then we might imagine space-time two dimensionally, as a taut sheet of rubber rather like a trampoline. A heavy bowling ball placed in its middle would, of course, cause a deep sag. A golf ball rolling by would be diverted from its straight path and start to orbit the bowling ball in its depression. In the universe, space-time is warped in a similar way, which is why the moon orbits the earth and the earth, in its turn, orbits the sun. This is true not only of objects but of light passing near heavenly bodies. The result of Einstein's calculations was a paper called "The Foundation of the General Theory of Relativity," published in the March 1916 issue of *Annalen der Physik*.

After this mental voyage in space, Einstein was exhausted but excited. It was a little while before he could bring his mind back to earth and give some attention to his sons. Switzerland was a neutral country, so Einstein was permitted to visit his family. He decided to go for the Easter holiday, but should have known it was not likely to be a peaceful vacation because in February he had written to Mileva asking for a divorce. When he wanted to take Hans Albert on a mountain hike, she objected strongly, and the two had a violent quarrel. Albert returned to Berlin and wrote a letter to his friend Michele Besso in which he swore he would never see his wife again. Soon afterward, Mileva had a nervous breakdown. Besso tried, unsuccessfully, to persuade Einstein to be more sympathetic to Mileva and to be a better father to Hans Albert and Eduard.

Back in Berlin, Einstein again buried himself in his work. All of his energy went into producing ten scientific papers and a book on relativity. He paid almost no attention to his health. He often failed to go to bed when he needed sleep, and the effects of his irregular eating habits were exaggerated by wartime food shortages. On one occasion, a visitor found Einstein attempting to boil an egg in a pot of soup to save time and minimize kitchen mess. In 1917, he developed several illnesses, including jaundice, a stomach ulcer, and severe depression. Finally, he collapsed in exhaustion.

Albert and Elsa Einstein, arriving in New York by ship.

CHAPTER FIVE

CELEBRITY

It was a lucky thing for Einstein and for twentieth-century science that Elsa Lowenthal and her two daughters happened to be living in Berlin in the fall of 1917. For several months, she brought him hot soup and nursed him when he was so sick he could hardly get out of bed. He lost more than fifty pounds. Because of his overwhelming fear that he was dying of cancer, he insisted on working and on maintaining his prewar contacts with English and French physicists through scientists in neutral countries.

Albert's recuperation was slow, and in the spring of 1918 he had a relapse. Elsa had a new concern. Even though she was functioning as a nurse, she was afraid that there would be gossip about all the time she spent alone with her patient. This would be bad for her daughters, who were reaching marriageable age. It is not clear who first made the suggestion, but Albert and Elsa were now discussing marriage.

During that summer, Albert again asked Mileva for a divorce. He promised to give her all of the thirty-two thousand dollars he would get from the Nobel Prize that he assumed he would eventually receive. In those days, the sum would have been enough of a fortune to support Mileva and the boys, so she agreed. The one hitch was that he had not yet been awarded the Nobel Prize. He had, however, been nominated for it six times since 1910. A scientist familiar with the award process later reported that the reason Einstein had not been given the prize for his work in relativity was that no scientists on the award committee could follow his calculations. Not only would they be embarrassed to give a prize for something they did not understand but it would be even worse if the theory were later disproved. To most people, including Mileva, it seemed only a matter of time before Einstein would get a Nobel Prize.

On November 11, 1918, the war ended, although there was still political turmoil in Germany. In February 1919, Mileva and Albert were divorced, and in June he and Elsa were married in a very simple ceremony. Einstein moved into the comfortable apartment that Elsa shared with her daughters. They would have to get used to him. Being surrounded by beautiful paintings, elegant furniture, and oriental carpets had no effect on Einstein's eccentric ways. Once, after he had spent more than an hour in the bathroom, Elsa's daughter Margot called to him to see if he was all right. He had been thinking through a problem while sitting in the bathtub. "I thought I was sitting at my desk," he said.

As soon as the war was over, Arthur Eddington, a British astronomer, organized two expeditions to photograph starlight during an eclipse of the sun in May 1919. The purpose of both trips was to prove one of Einstein's predictions in his theory of general relativity. One group went to northern Brazil. The other, led by Eddington him-

Albert and Elsa at home in Berlin.

self, went to an island off the coast of west Africa. Clouds forced Eddington to return with only one clear picture out of the sixteen glass-plate photographs taken. The first ones from Brazil were not much better, but the last seven exposures, along with Eddington's one, confirmed that Einstein's theory was right. Starlight did bend while passing the sun. Gravity affects light.

On November 6, 1919, there was a joint meeting of two prestigious British scientific organizations, the Royal Society and the Royal
Astronomical Society. A portrait of Sir Isaac Newton gazed over the
gathering of eminent scientists. J. J. Thomson, discoverer of electrons,
small particles that revolve around the nucleus of an atom, explained
the significance of Eddington's work. He said it demonstrated that
Einstein's theory was "the greatest discovery in connection with gravitation since Newton." But he also pointed out that "no one has yet
succeeded in stating in clear language what the theory of Einstein
really is."

J. J. Thomson,
discoverer of electrons.

Radio was not yet fully established as a commercial news medium, but a storm of misinformation gradually mushroomed in the press. It began the next day on page twelve of the London *Times* with the headline "Revolution in Science. Newtonian Ideas Overthrown." Einstein had always insisted that his own work was simply an extension of Newton's concepts, an evolution, not a revolution, but the confusion multiplied in newspapers across England and around the world. The writer assigned to cover the story for the respected British paper the *Manchester Guardian* was its music critic, and the only reporter available in England for the *New York Times* was a sportswriter. In mid-December, a picture of Einstein appeared in the German magazine *Berliner Illustrirte Zeitung* with the caption "A new figure in world history whose investigations signify a complete revision of nature." Hardly anyone, including many leading scientists, actually understood Einstein's theory.

Even though some scientists said the general theory of relativity was nonsense, Einstein was becoming a world renowned celebrity. A theory proposed by a German physicist had been proven correct by an English astronomer. Perhaps two countries that had been enemies only a year before could again cooperate scientifically. Exhausted by a war more devastating than any in history, people desperately wanted to believe in the renewal of peace and harmony. Einstein became a symbol of hope for the future. Whether he was ready or not, the public was rapidly intruding upon Einstein's private world of science.

Personal problems also intruded. In January 1920, Pauline Einstein, who was dying of stomach cancer, moved in to spend the final months of her life with her son. Albert let her use his study as her sickroom and moved his work to a small attic room. Elsa helped care for her mother-in-law, but the stressful situation did not last long, as Pauline died only a month after she settled in.

Einstein found it difficult to concentrate during his mother's painful illness and her death upset him, but he could not ignore the alarming political developments going on around him in Berlin. The defeat of Germany in the world war had caused widespread unemployment and galloping inflation, which in turn led to the encouragement of extremist political parties. Left-wing members of the Communist Party fought in the streets with right-wing nationalists of the National Socialist German Workers, or Nazi, Party. Most alarming of all was the rising tide of anti-Semitism. Many Germans began to believe the creeping rumors that Jews had caused the defeat of the German army. It was claimed that they were unpatriotic and had even stabbed frontline soldiers in the back. According to Einstein biographer Denis Brian, "Ironically, German Jews had been fervent patriots; a higher percentage of Jews than non-Jews had served in the German military, and twelve thousand had been killed in action." Nevertheless, more and more Germans were being caught up in the fever of hatred.

As a prominent Jew whose reputation was growing, Einstein was bound to become a target of anti-Semitism. He was booed at some of his lectures, and threatening notes were often stuffed in his university mailbox. At first, Einstein tried to keep a low profile by leaving Berlin once in a while. In May 1920, he visited a friend, Paul Ehrenfest, at the University of Leiden in the Netherlands. In June, he went to give lectures in Norway and Denmark. On this trip he met the Danish physicist Niels Bohr, who had worked on the application of Planck's quantum theory to atomic structure and who would later help with research for the atomic bomb.

Back in Berlin in August, Einstein and Walther Nernst went to a rally and debate that had been scheduled by fellow physicist Philipp Lenard for the sole purpose of discrediting Albert Einstein. It was sponsored by an anti-Semitic and antipacifist organization that Einstein nicknamed "the Anti-Relativity Company." Einstein sometimes attended such rallies as a sort of entertainment. At this one he laughed when he heard himself denounced as a fake, and he applauded sarcastically at statements suggesting that he had stolen some of his ideas from an Aryan or non-Jewish scientist. He appeared to be amused, but afterward Einstein wrote an angry letter that was published in a Berlin newspaper. Anti-Semitism was no laughing matter. In fact, it had begun to hurt deeply.

How could Einstein respond to the hurt? Nazi-inspired hatred of him was doubled by his pacifism. The National Socialists believed that both pacifists and Jews had caused Germany's defeat in the war, and for Einstein pacifism was a gut feeling. In his biography, Philipp Frank quotes a remark Einstein made in 1920: "My pacifism is an instinctive feeling, a feeling that possesses me because the murder of men is disgusting."

Passive pacifism is, however, helpless in the face of aggressive hostility. As Mohandas Gandhi had already shown in South Africa and would later demonstrate in India, some sort of nonviolent resistance is the only response available to the dedicated pacifist. Even though Einstein was not a strictly religious person, he felt a spiritual connection to the predicament of his fellow Jews, who were becoming unwelcome in their own homelands in Europe. His growing international reputation would eventually offer him a chance to do something for them. "The public wondered what sort of man was this Einstein," wrote Philipp Frank, "and they wanted to see and hear this

Mohandas Gandhi in 1915. Einstein and Gandhi both knew the frustrations faced by truly committed pacifists.

famous scientist in person. From every country, Einstein began to receive invitations to come and give lectures."

Frank had taken Einstein's old job at the German University in Prague. When Einstein went there to lecture, he stayed with Frank and his new wife, also a scientist. Because housing was hard to find in postwar Prague, the couple was living temporarily in the physics laboratories, where the scientists did their cooking on the gas-fired Bunsen burners used for experiments. One day they planned liver for lunch. When Einstein saw Mrs. Frank about to boil the liver in water, he jumped up. "What are you doing there?" he said. "You certainly know that the boiling point of water is too low to be able to fry liver in it. You must use a substance with a higher boiling point such as butter or fat." For the rest of their lives, whenever the subject of Einstein's theories came up, the Franks would amuse people with Einstein's theory of cooking liver.

The liver-cooking theory was perhaps all that many people were able to understand. The evening following that lunch in the laboratory, Einstein gave a lecture to an enthusiastic throng in an overcrowded auditorium. "Einstein spoke as simply and clearly as possible," reported Frank. "But the public was much too excited to understand the meaning of the lecture." When Einstein went on to Vienna, he spoke to a crowd of three thousand people. "Even more than in Prague, the public was in . . . the kind of mental state in which it no longer matters what one understands so long as one is in the immediate neighborhood of a place where miracles are happening."

When he returned to Berlin, Einstein discovered that he was attracting more attention than ever. No matter how hard he tried to clarify his theories, they were involved in increasing controversy. Some scientists attacked them out of professional jealously and others because they honestly did not understand them. National Socialists attacked them because they were the work of a Jew. Many people were working hard to make Einstein's life uncomfortable so he would leave Germany, but the government wanted him to stay because his international reputation brought honor to the country. In fact, he might have left if Max Planck had not persuaded him to stay in Berlin.

In January 1921, Einstein was offered a chance to take a break from the tumult of German politics. He was invited to accompany

Chaim Weizmann to the United States on a fundraising trip for the Zionist cause. Weizmann was a Russian-born chemist who had worked in England during the war as director of the Admiralty Laboratories, developing explosives for the navy. Toward the end of the war, he had managed to persuade the British government that there was a serious need for a Jewish homeland. In 1917, foreign minister Arthur James Balfour, a former prime minister, who earlier in the war had been First Lord of the Admiralty, sponsored the Balfour Declaration. This was a pledge that the British government supported the Zionist efforts to establish a Jewish state in Palestine, provided the rights of non-Jews were respected.

Weizmann now planned to make a tour of U.S. cities to develop political support and raise millions of dollars for the project. Einstein

Chaim Weizmann, who invited the Einsteins to join him on a tour of the United States to raise money for the Zionist cause and for the founding of Hebrew University in Jerusalem.

had never been strongly attracted to Zionism and did not think it had much chance of success now. The thing that interested him about Weizmann's invitation was that the plans for a Jewish homeland included a Hebrew university in Jerusalem. In recent years, universities throughout Europe had begun rejecting Jewish applicants simply because they were Jews. Einstein thought that Jewish students deserved their own institution where they could get a good education.

On April 1, 1921, Elsa and Albert Einstein with Vera and Chaim Weizmann arrived in New York aboard the Dutch ocean liner *Rotterdam*. Even before they got off the ship, they were surrounded by reporters and photographers who bombarded them with questions and asked Einstein to define relativity in a few sentences. "If you will not take the answer too seriously," he said, "and consider it as a kind of joke, then I can explain it as follows. It was formerly believed that if all material things disappeared out of the universe, only time and space would be left. According to the relativity theory, however, time and space disappear together with the things." Finally, he concluded the interview by saying, "Well, gentlemen, I hope I have passed my examination." Then it was Elsa's turn. When asked if she understood the theory of relativity, she answered, "Oh no, although he has explained it to me so many times. But it is not necessary to my happiness."

When the Weizmanns and the Einsteins got off the boat, Einstein was wearing a wing collar, a scruffy overcoat, and a broad-brimmed black hat. He carried his pipe in one hand and a violin case in the other. "He looked like an artist," wrote one reporter, "a musician." The two couples got in their car and found themselves caught up in a horn-honking motorcade, escorted by mounted police, that moved them slowly through the streets of Manhattan. After crawling through the wildly cheering Jewish section on the Lower East Side, the parade went on for hours before they finally got to their hotel. When they went inside, they were followed by a flock of reporters, and Einstein was again subjected to a barrage of questions. At last he had a chance to ask his own question. Why was the public so fascinated with a middle-aged scientist whose theories they did not understand? Then he offered an answer to his own question. "The ladies of New York want to have a new style every year. This year the fashion is relativity."

Throughout April and May, the Weizmanns and the Einsteins visited Boston, Chicago, Cleveland, Princeton, and Washington, D.C., frequently returning to New York. At Columbia University, Einstein gave a lecture in German, as his English was still elementary. At Harvard, he helped graduate students with their physics problems. At Princeton, he lectured and was awarded an honorary degree. In Washington, they met President Warren G. Harding and attended the annual dinner of the National Academy of Sciences. The evening was burdened with one long, boring speech after another. Finally, Einstein turned to the person next to him and said, "I have just got a new theory of eternity." In Boston, he was informed that the famous inventor Thomas Edison disapproved of the liberal arts curriculum offered in colleges because it did not teach the facts that one needed to get along in the practical world. Edison believed that colleges should teach only facts. He had even made up a list of 150 factual questions to give to job applicants. Einstein disagreed with this point of view. "A person doesn't need to go to college to learn facts," he asserted. "He can get them from books. The value of a college education is that it trains the mind to think. And that's something you can't learn from textbooks."

*President Warren G. Harding,
whom the Einsteins met on
their fundraising tour of the
United States in 1921.*

The main point of the trip, however, was to raise money for the Jewish National Fund and the Hebrew University. Weizmann was the leader. Einstein regarded himself as an exotic trophy brought along to attract attention. At one gathering of eight thousand people he was asked to speak after Weizmann had given a speech. He stood and faced the audience. "Your leader, Dr. Weizmann, has spoken," said Einstein, "and he has spoken very well for us all. Follow him and you will do well. That is all I have to say."

On the whole, the tour was a success. The fundraising efforts brought in $4 million, not quite as much as had been hoped for but enough to get started on Hebrew University. The Einsteins headed home with a pile of household gadgets they had bought in Woolworth's five-and-ten-cent stores and four cases of ginger ale, which was not available in Europe. On the way back, they stopped

briefly in England, where Einstein's world fame had begun only a year
and a half before with the report of Eddington's findings to the Royal
Society. They met Prime Minister David Lloyd George and many
other famous Britons. At Westminster Abbey in London, Einstein
placed a wreath on Isaac Newton's grave, and at Oxford University,
Professor Frederick Lindemann gave them a guided tour of the
physics labs. They returned to Berlin able to speak better English than
they could two months earlier.

Life in Berlin was just as tense as it had been when the Einsteins
left, but they attempted to ignore the strain. After a July vacation in
Switzerland with his two sons, Einstein returned to his teaching

*Prime Minister David
Lloyd George, whom
the Einsteins met in
England on their way
home from their U.S.
tour.*

duties. His students particularly liked his informal way of working with them. Unlike other stiff and distant professors, he treated everyone as an equal. One student, a Hungarian named Leo Szilard, who was working on his Ph.D. thesis, found Einstein most helpful. Einstein liked Szilard's way of thinking. Instead of working intensely on a narrow subject, Szilard was able to gather information from many fields and blend ideas together. Student and teacher formed a strong enough relationship that they could argue vehemently over theories and formulas without breaking the bond that existed between them.

The academic world could not, however, ignore the political trouble that was brewing in Europe. In January 1922, Einstein went to Paris to give two lectures. In France, where the war had been especially horrible, there was still a lot of hatred for the Germans. The Paris police feared that a crowd gathering at the train station Gare du Nord might be hostile to Einstein, and there was tight security for his lecture at the College de France. Those present were charmed by his halting French, but another speech scheduled for the French Academy of Sciences was canceled when thirty of its members threatened to walk out in protest if he appeared. When Einstein returned to Berlin, many of his scientific colleagues avoided him because he had spoken in France.

On a sunny summer day in June 1922, Walther Rathenau, the German foreign minister, was riding in an open car when another car pulled alongside. Two young men with submachine guns sprayed him with bullets and then threw a hand grenade into the car. In her biography of Einstein, Elsa's friend Antonina Vallentin, who was a correspondent for the *Manchester Guardian*, wrote, "The murderers knew nothing about their victim, except that he was a Jew."

Einstein had been a friend of Rathenau's and had advised him not to accept the government appointment. He was shocked by the assassination. Although he was concerned about the rumors circulating in Berlin that he was next, he did not think precautions were necessary for his own safety on a train trip to Holland to give a lecture. His wife, on the other hand, was terrified. "She saw death lying in wait for him," wrote Vallentin. "He never knew . . . that Elsa had persuaded the chief of police to keep a close watch . . . that the row of men on the platform were plainclothes policemen, and that the two young men who got into the compartment with him, their hands pushed into their pockets, had undertaken to deliver him safe and sound."

When he returned to Germany, anti-Semitism seemed to have become worse. "I cannot stay in Berlin," Einstein wrote in a letter to Marie Curie, "as threats have already been made on my life. . . . I shall take this as an excuse to move away from turbulent Berlin to somewhere quiet where I am able to work." He had already canceled a lecture he was to have given in Berlin, and later he canceled another scheduled for Leipzig.

He had also agreed to other lectures, but these were at safe distances. On October 8, 1922, in Marseilles, Albert and Elsa boarded the Japanese ship *Kitano Maru* bound for Kobe, Japan. Along the way the Einsteins visited Ceylon, now known as Sri Lanka. Einstein wrote in his diary that he was ashamed to have to get around town in rickshaws, "small one-man carriages drawn at a trot by men of Herculean strength yet delicate build." The next ports of call were Singapore, Hong Kong, Shanghai, and finally Kobe. In their own way, the Japanese greeted Einstein with as much enthusiasm as the Americans had. His first lecture, including the translations from

German, lasted four hours. Thinking the patient audience must have had difficulty understanding the material, Einstein shortened his lecture so that the next event took only two and a half hours. Later, a nervous Japanese explained politely that the second audience had felt insulted that the speech given them was shorter than the one delivered to the first audience.

The Einsteins loved the Japanese and their culture, and they were sad when it was time to sail home from Tokyo. After a few days at sea, their ship received a radio message: The Swedish Academy of Sciences, which had still not awarded the 1921 prize in physics to anyone, had now, in 1922, decided to give it to Albert Einstein.

When Berlin hosted the 1936 Olympic games, Hitler used the occasion to create propaganda for the Nazi government.

CHAPTER SIX

SCIENCE AND TOTALITARIANISM

The Nobel award committee had found a way to avoid the controversy surrounding the theory of relativity. They awarded the prize to Einstein "for his services to Theoretical Physics and especially for his discovery of the law of photoelectric effect." By the 1920s, the concept of the photoelectric effect that Einstein had explained in 1905 was in practical use. It was fundamental to the invention of the photoelectric cell, or phototube, a critical part of television that was being developed in laboratories, although it would not be commercially available until 1945.

Nevertheless, the award inspired controversy. The anti-Semitic physicist Philipp Lenard accused the Swedish Academy of making an award for something that was not particularly significant just to strengthen Einstein's reputation. The German and Swiss embassies in Sweden got into intense discussions over which country could claim Einstein as a citizen. Perhaps it was just as well that Einstein was unable to receive the award in person because he was on the high seas returning home from Tokyo. The German ambassador to Sweden accepted the award in Stockholm on his behalf. Later, the Swiss ambassador to Germany would deliver it to Einstein when he returned to Berlin.

Meanwhile, Albert and Elsa had interrupted their trip home to tour Palestine. Einstein made a speech in Jerusalem at the cornerstone that had been laid for the future Hebrew University, planted a tree on Mount Carmel, and visited a kibbutz in Tel Aviv. They went on to Spain, where he gave lectures at Barcelona and Madrid and then took a train for Berlin. The luxurious royal coach of King Alfonso XIII of Spain was hooked to the train for the Einsteins' travel comfort. Albert hated it and told Elsa she could travel however she wanted, but in the future he would always travel third class.

Anti-Semitism in Germany was as virulent as ever and getting worse. Partly to confuse his enemies, Einstein continued his occasional excursions. In July 1923, he went to Sweden to give a lecture in place of the acceptance speech he would have given if he had been able to attend the Nobel Prize ceremonies. He sent the cash part of the award to Mileva to support herself and the two boys. Several times that summer, he took the train to Zurich to see Hans Albert and Eduard. The boys, each in his own way, had come to resent their father's absence. Once, Einstein thought of bringing Hans Albert to live in Berlin, but Mileva had vetoed the idea. Eduard, the more sensitive of the two, had seemed mentally disturbed ever since the age of seven, and Einstein was paying for his treatments at a children's clinic. In between visits to his sons, he found the time to write and publish two articles on his work toward the unified field theory, an effort to establish a common basis for general relativity and quantum theory.

During 1923, uncontrollable inflation led to widespread economic hardship for millions of Germans. Academic salaries were severely cut. Einstein, however, survived comfortably on his salaries from the Prussian Academy of Sciences, the Kaiser Wilhelm Gesell-schaft, and the University of Berlin, plus royalties from his popular book on relativity. But the increasing hunger and misery inspired the Nazis to escalate their struggle for political power. In September, they started a false rumor that Einstein would soon give a lecture in Moscow, where the Bolshevik Revolution had established a Communist government of Russia. Linking him with their archenemies was intended to fan the flames of anti-Semitic hatred.

In November, the Nazis made their first grab for national dominance. At a rally in a beer hall in Munich, Adolf Hitler jumped onto a table, fired a revolver at the ceiling, and yelled, "The National Revolution has begun!" The next day he led three thousand brown-shirted Nazis into town, smashed the presses of a local newspaper, and started a riot. The police broke it up by shooting into the mob. Hitler escaped but was arrested a few days later. With Hitler sentenced to five years in prison, some people in Germany hoped that the Nazis might lose momentum and become an insignificant splinter party.

For most of 1924, Einstein remained in Berlin, but his fame now brought the world to him. He had become a major tourist attraction. When he gave a lecture at the university, the auditorium would often be jammed with people who had come just to see the great man. Philipp Frank wrote that on these occasions Einstein would start the lecture and then pause. "I shall now stop for a few minutes so that those with no further interest can leave," he would say. When the tourists were gone, there would be fewer than a dozen serious students left to participate in the study of physics.

At home, Elsa and her daughters had to keep visitors from intruding on Einstein's work. He also depended in other ways on Elsa, who sometimes functioned more like a mother than a wife. She had to keep track of his money and restrict him to small allowances when he went out because he was likely to give everything in his pockets to anyone who happened to say he needed money. When he was working, Albert had to be reminded to get his sleep. He and Elsa then went to separate bedrooms at opposite ends of their apartment. Supposedly, this was because he snored thunderously, but it was also because he often wandered around at night, sometimes to make notes, sometimes to play the violin in the kitchen. In the daytime he drifted absent-mindedly through the house, from his desk to the piano and back. He was

Einstein playing the violin.

unaware of household schedules, ate only when food was placed in front of him, and appeared befuddled if someone spoke to him. When Einstein was thinking about physics, he was oblivious to the world around him.

In 1924, much of this work focused on quantum theory. A young physicist named Satyenda Bose of Dacca University in India had sent Einstein a paper explaining a new way of arriving at Planck's equation by thinking of photons, or units of light, as particles. Light waves could now be described in terms of particles. Einstein reasoned that if this was so, then the reverse was also true. Light particles could be described in terms of waves. By 1925, he had completed a paper describing the wave-particle nature of light. He credited a French graduate student named Louis de Broglie, who the year before had written a Ph.D. thesis in which he arrived at the same description by a totally different method. De Broglie is now considered the father of the concept of the dual nature of light, but no one would have heard of either de Broglie or Bose if they had not been publicized through Einstein's international reputation.

Although Einstein studied numerous aspects of quantum theory, it was consolidated by Niels Bohr of Denmark. Working in his research laboratory in Copenhagen, Bohr, along with another physicist, Werner Heisenberg, established the uncertainty principle. The two scientists maintained that the very act of measuring particles changes them in such a way that it is impossible to predict their behavior. Einstein was unable to accept the uncertainty in quantum theory. He thought that there was predictability in all things if we could only discover it. This led to a long-running debate with Bohr. Einstein's point of view is summed up in his now famous statement, "God does not play dice with the universe."

Physicists were not the only thinkers Einstein was interested in. When Sigmund Freud, the seventy-year-old father of psychoanalysis, came to Berlin in January 1927, Elsa and Albert visited him. After a two-hour discussion about psychology and physics, Freud concluded that, in contrast to his own pioneering work, Einstein's path had been made easy by predecessors beginning with Newton. Einstein came away from the conversation deeply suspicious of psychoanalytic therapy. He later remarked that he would prefer to "remain in the darkness of not having been analyzed." Although Freud was by this time in his life quite hard of hearing, he may have had a more balanced summary of the meeting between two of the most influential thinkers

Dr. Sigmund Freud, father of psychoanalysis, met Elsa and Albert Einstein in 1927.

of the twentieth century. "Einstein," he said, "understands as much about psychology as I do about physics."

In 1928, Einstein's personal life took several unpredictable turns. The first was the death of his old friend, mentor, and admirer, Hendrick Lorentz. In 1895, the Dutch physicist had laid part of the foundation for Einstein's special theory of relativity when he developed theories about the interrelationships of magnetism, electricity, and light. Physicist Abraham Pais, Einstein's friend and biographer, wrote, "Einstein's thoughts and feelings about Lorentz were a blend of respect, love, and awe." As one of the speakers at the funeral, Einstein expressed his gratitude for Lorentz's life as a brilliant scientist and generous human being. Many years later, near the end of his own life, Einstein wrote of Lorentz, "Everything that emanated from this supremely great mind was as clear and beautiful as a good work of art."

In February, Einstein collapsed on his way back to Germany after giving a lecture in Davos, Switzerland. The diagnosis was inflammation of the walls of the heart. Einstein was put to bed for several weeks. He was kept on a salt-free diet and forbidden to smoke his beloved pipe. The extra work of looking after a bedridden patient added to dealing with the daily correspondence that now flooded the Einstein household was too much for Elsa. She decided to look for a secretary and found the sister of a friend. At first, Helen Dukas was afraid even to meet Einstein. Elsa assured her that he was kind to everyone and that a knowledge of physics was not needed to qualify for the job. Einstein put her at ease as soon as they met, and Helen Dukas remained his secretary for the next twenty-seven years.

Einstein was almost entirely recovered by the date of his fiftieth birthday, March 14, 1929. "Greetings arrived from all parts of the world," wrote Antonina Vallentin. "Telegrams came in such numbers that they were delivered in laundry baskets. Masses of presents arrived . . . gifts from millionaires and offerings from the humble." Perhaps the best present was from a group of friends and students who gave him an elegant new sailboat to replace the leaky old tub in which he had been spending leisure time on the string of lakes formed by the Havel River. Sailing was now a form of relaxation as important to him as playing the violin.

Einstein aboard the sailboat given him by friends and students on his fiftieth birthday.

In an effort to avoid the excitement, Einstein had fled a few days before to a cottage on the country estate of a friend. Elsa was to join him for a quiet lunch. Early in the day, he telephoned her to explain about an error in some calculations he had left with his assistant. Elsa asked him if he knew what day it was. "He did not know," reported Vallentin. "He had forgotten what he had run away from. When his wife reminded him, he burst out laughing. 'Such a lot of fuss over a birthday. But don't forget what I told you.' And he put down the receiver."

The city council of Berlin wanted to honor Einstein with the gift of a country home on the Havel River, but when Elsa went to look at it, she found it already leased to some people who did not intend to move. The embarrassed council then offered him a piece of land on which he could build a house, but it turned out that local zoning regulations did not permit building on that particular parcel of land. Finally, the council said that the Einsteins could search for whatever real estate they liked and the council would buy it for them. In the village of Caputh, Elsa found a piece she knew would please Albert, and she hired their architect friend Konrad Wachsmann to draw plans for a small house. At this point, a Nazi sympathizer on the council said that it was inappropriate for the city to make such a gift. Einstein sent a curt letter to the mayor of Berlin. "My life is too short for me to adapt myself to your methods," he wrote. "I thank you for your friendly intentions. Now, however, my birthday is already past and I decline the gift." The Einsteins then sank all their savings into buying the land themselves and building their dream vacation house.

The cottage in Caputh was a simple and comfortable dwelling, and Einstein could work there as well as in Berlin. In both places he found that the life of a celebrity could be amusing, especially when

Elsa in the living room of the Einsteins' country house in Caputh.

young women were attracted to the world-renowned scientist. He enjoyed flirting with them, and one wealthy Viennese woman used to take him to the opera in her limousine, leaving Elsa at home. The Einsteins' friend Konrad Wachsmann said that probably there was nothing physical about Albert's various relationships with the young ladies. Understandably, however, these liaisons were not at all amusing to Elsa. In fact, they upset her considerably, and sometimes even her daughters were involved in the family arguments about her husband's thoughtless behavior.

Trouble even more painful than family quarrels was brewing in Germany. Hitler had been released after serving only nine months of the five-year term to which he had been sentenced in 1923. He had spent his time in prison dictating his personal memoir called *Mein*

*Adolf Hitler
in the early 1930s.*

Kampf (My Struggle). The book was filled with anger and hatred and outlined a strategy for the Germans to seize power and dominate the world. Under Hitler's leadership, the Nazi Party had been growing steadily, and with the worldwide financial crash of 1929, it gained the support of millions.

The Nazi philosophy of Germanic or Aryan supremacy was gaining strength, and efforts were being made to "cleanse" the universities of non-Aryan teachers. Philipp Frank points out that explaining who was Aryan and who was not was hardly a logical process. "There was no scientific definition of an 'Aryan,'" wrote Frank, "except that he was a person who spoke a language belonging to the 'Aryan linguistic family.' Such a definition, however, was impossible; otherwise everyone who spoke Yiddish, which is basically a German dialect, would be an Aryan." So the concept of Aryan superiority had to be based on who was non-Aryan. That was defined by the Nazis as anyone who had at least one Jewish grandparent. There were other peoples with whom the Nazis wanted to be friendly who did not fit their definition of non-Aryan. Hungarians and Arabs could not be called either Aryans or non-Aryans. The same was true of the Japanese, with whom the Nazis were later allied. This called for a new category, which Frank says could only be described as "non-non-Aryan."

In the universities, Nazi students instigated noisy protests against Jewish teachers. There was also a hate campaign in which Einstein was accused of being the leader of a Communist conspiracy to take over Germany. In general, however, research scientists were not yet under direct attack, and Einstein managed to increase his safety margin by going abroad to give lectures.

Through the efforts of the American physicist Robert Millikan, the Einsteins spent the winter of 1930–1931 at the California Institute of Technology in Pasadena. Scientists, even conservatives like Millikan himself, were glad to have him as a visiting professor at Caltech. Some nonscientists, however, were afraid Einstein would poison the minds of students with his Zionist and pacifist views. Nevertheless, the visit was a success, and Einstein worked with Edwin Hubble, head of the group of astronomers who ran the Mount Wilson Observatory, home of the most powerful telescope in the world.

After returning to Germany in the spring, Albert and Elsa were off again. This time they went to Oxford University, where Einstein's old friend Frederick Lindemann had arranged for him to deliver a series of lectures at Christ Church College. Lindemann wanted Einstein to have

Einstein takes a break from his work at Caltech.

a permanent position at Oxford. At first, a research fellowship for him at Christ Church College was opposed by several liberal arts professors, including a few who were anti-Semitic. The proposal passed, however, and Einstein received an appointment to spend a small part of each of the next five years at Oxford doing research in physics.

Einstein spent as little time as possible in Berlin. When he was in Germany, he preferred to work in the peaceful and woodsy setting of the cottage at Caputh. It was here in the summer of 1932 that he was visited by Abraham Flexner. The two had already met in Pasadena and again at Oxford. The purpose of Flexner's visit was to interest Einstein in a new institution, a center for advanced study to be founded at Princeton University in New Jersey.

The idea was to gather prominent scientists from around the world to live at the institute and carry on their research in any way they chose with no required teaching or lecturing responsibilities. Whenever they felt like it, they might hold seminars for students who had already earned their Ph.D.'s. The project was funded by a five-million-dollar gift from two philanthropists, Louis Bamberger and his sister Mrs. Felix Fuld. In the course of the eight-hour discussion, Einstein became enthusiastic about the idea. Later, in a letter to Flexner, he accepted with the understanding that he would have to spend half the year at the University of Berlin. He did not want to leave his colleagues or his charming little cottage by the Havelsee. Asked to name his own salary, Einstein suggested three thousand dollars, which Flexner said was not enough to live on. In the end, Flexner and Elsa settled on sixteen thousand dollars with a pension after retirement and payments to Elsa if Einstein died. In 1932, this was a generous financial arrangement.

Meanwhile, Hitler's poison was spreading rapidly throughout Germany. Even in rural Caputh there were anti-Semitic villagers. In December 1932, the Einsteins were getting ready to travel for their third winter at Caltech. As they were leaving their country home, Albert told Elsa to have a good look at it. When she asked why, he replied, "You will never see it again." Elsa thought Albert was being overly dramatic.

In the spring of 1933, the little house in Caputh was searched by Nazi police and the garden was dug up. They were looking for guns and ammunition they were sure had been stored there in preparation for a Communist revolt. The Einsteins' Berlin bank account was confiscated on the grounds that it was going to be used to help finance the revolt, and the Berlin apartment was raided several times by storm troopers.

The news of these events reached Albert and Elsa while they were sailing home to Germany after their third winter in Pasadena. Einstein immediately decided that when the ship docked at Antwerp in Belgium, he and Elsa would not go on to Germany. In a public statement he said, "These acts are the result of the government's overnight transfer of police powers to a raw and rabid mob of the Nazi militia. My summer home has often in the past been honored by the presence of guests. . . . No one had any reason to break in."

Late in January 1933, Hitler had been appointed chancellor of Germany by the aging and popular President Paul von Hindenburg, hero of World War I. No one, including Einstein, had imagined that Hitler's rise to national power would be so swift. Only a few months earlier, he had lost the presidential election to Hindenburg by a wide margin. Political turmoil had escalated, and some people in the fragile government thought Hitler was the only person who could stand up to the Communists. Although Hindenburg's position as president was mostly ceremonial, it included the responsibility for appointing government officials. The chancellor was the chief executive officer of the government.

In February, the Nazis secretly set fire to the building that housed the Reichstag, the German national legislature, and publicly blamed it on the Communists to inflate political hysteria. In the March elections, the National Socialist Party won a slender majority in the Reichstag, the Communists were outlawed, and Hitler was given dictatorial powers. On April 1, police prevented customers from entering Jewish shops, and many of the stores were trashed by storm

Hitler on tour.

troopers. A month later, in a public square near the university, truck-loads of books were burned by screaming mobs. The authors whose works were destroyed included such modern writers as Sigmund Freud, Helen Keller, Ernest Hemingway, and Albert Einstein. Hitler would soon consolidate his power by having the Reichstag eliminate the state governments, outlaw all political parties except the Nazis, and combine the two offices of president and chancellor into one.

Meanwhile, Albert and Elsa settled in the small seaside village of Le Coq-sur-Mer near the port of Ostend in Belgium. Almost immediately, Einstein issued a public statement that began, "As long as I have any choice, I will only stay in a country where political liberty, toleration, and equality of all citizens before the law are the rule. . . . These conditions do not obtain in Germany at the present time." He went on to hope that "healthy conditions" would soon prevail. For the time being, however, he could not live in Germany under its present government. In fact, if he had tried to return to Berlin and Caputh, he probably would have been murdered.

To make his separation from Nazi Germany absolutely clear, Einstein resigned from the Prussian Academy. In a public declaration, the academy responded that it was indignant over Einstein's "atrocity-mongering" and his "activities as an agitator in foreign countries. . . . It has therefore no reason to regret Einstein's withdrawal." This produced a brisk exchange of denials and new accusations between Einstein and the permanent secretary of the academy. In a final letter to Einstein, the secretary said that he had hoped that "one who had belonged to our Academy for so long would have ranged himself . . . on the side of the defenders of our nation against the flood of lies which has been let loose upon it. . . . A good word for the German people from you in particular might have produced a great effect, especially abroad." Einstein answered that a good word from him "would only have helped the cause of those who are seeking to undermine the ideas and principles which have won for the German nation a place of honor in the civilized world. . . . It was for this reason that I felt compelled to resign from the Academy, and your letter only shows me how right I was to do so."

Life was quiet and comfortable among the sand dunes of Le Coq, where Elsa's daughters, Ilse and Margot, had joined them. So had two bodyguards assigned by King Albert I and Queen Elizabeth of Belgium, who were concerned about rumors of assassination. The Einsteins had picked the village hoping it would be hard for both friends and enemies to discover them. Nevertheless, many strangers appeared. Philipp Frank managed to locate the house, but as he approached it the two

Philipp Frank, biographer and fellow physicist, with Einstein.

bodyguards tackled him and did not let him up until a terrified Elsa finally recognized him.

Frank had become a fellow refugee and would eventually find his way to the United States to take a position at Harvard. In his biography of Einstein, he compared the situation to a bargain basement. The non-Aryan teachers who had been let go from schools and universities in Germany were like "merchandise that had to be sold at reduced prices as 'irregulars.'. . . It was as if a great museum were suddenly to offer for sale Rembrandt's most valuable paintings at a very low price because the new directors of the museum did not like to have pictures of a certain style." Frederick Lindemann also found the Einsteins in Le Coq. He was bargain shopping around Europe, recruiting refugee scientists for Great Britain, but he was, of course, too late to sign up Einstein full time. There had already been other invitations from such institutions as the Sorbonne in Paris, Hebrew University, the University of Madrid, and Caltech. Although he was willing to spend summers at Oxford, Einstein was committed to Flexner's project in Princeton, New Jersey.

During his stay in Belgium, Einstein reached the conclusion that he had to modify his long-held position on pacifism. Asked to speak up for some Belgians who had refused military service, he wrote a letter to them stating that if the Germans were to occupy Belgium, the situation would be much worse than when they had done so in 1914. He therefore urged the conscientious objectors to join the army. Military opposition to the Nazis was the only hope of saving civilization. "This does not mean that I am surrendering the principle for which I have stood heretofore," he wrote. "I hope most sincerely that the time will once more come when refusal of military service will again be an effective method of serving the cause of human progress."

Pacifists everywhere felt betrayed by what they regarded as Einstein's about-face. Only those near him knew he had arrived at his conclusion through great pain. In general, he still believed that violence and warfare were morally wrong. In normal times, to avoid participating in violence would, he thought, advance humanity. But Einstein judged the effectiveness of principles by anticipating their consequences. In the present situation, to refrain from military service would only strengthen the Nazi cause. If no one stood up to them, he reasoned, the bullies would feel free to march anywhere they chose in Europe, or even the rest of the world.

Einstein in his study at home in Princeton.

CHAPTER SEVEN

ELDER STATESMAN
OF PHYSICS

The political scene of 1933 indicated that Einstein's days in Europe were numbered. He made a quick trip to Zurich to visit his younger son, Eduard. The older, Hans Albert, eventually became a professor of civil engineering in California, but Eduard had suffered a nervous breakdown three years earlier. He would spend the rest of his life in Zurich undergoing various types of mental therapy. Then Einstein went to England, where he told Winston Churchill that, in defiance of the peace treaty Germany had signed after World War I, Hitler was rearming the country. Returning to Belgium, he learned of a report stating that his name was at the top of the Nazis' death list and that there was a price on his head of five thousand dollars. Elsa was horrified at his casual response: "I didn't know I was worth that much."

Without telling her husband, Elsa managed to have a member of the British Parliament invite Albert back to England in support of a bill to help Jewish refugees in that country become British subjects. With a heavy escort of detectives from Scotland Yard, Einstein made a speech in London to help raise money in aid of the refugees from Germany. He spent most of the rest of his time in a lonely cottage on the windswept seacoast, well to the north of London, with a couple of detectives and a two bodyguards disguised as secretaries.

In October, Einstein boarded the ship *Westernland*, which had already brought Elsa and Helen Dukas from Antwerp, to sail across the Atlantic to New York. To avoid the huge welcoming crowd at the dock, Flexner had arranged for a launch to whisk them across New York Harbor to the New Jersey shore. In Princeton, Albert and Elsa settled first at a hotel, then a rented house, and eventually at 112 Mercer Street, where they would later be joined by Albert's beloved sister, Maja. Einstein's first public act in the United States was to buy a vanilla ice cream cone with chocolate sprinkles.

Einstein's sister, Maja, in Princeton, 1940.

In November, President Franklin D. Roosevelt invited Einstein to visit the White House. All of the mail to the institute was being handled by Flexner, who answered for Einstein, saying that a trip to Washington was far too dangerous as there was "an irresponsible group of Nazis" in New York. It is possible that Nazi spies in New York, only fifty miles from Princeton, could have been a threat to Einstein's travels. Flexner's main concern, however, was to keep tight control of the Institute for Advanced Study. He further explained that if Professor Einstein started accepting social invitations, it would be almost impossible for him to carry on the scientific work for which he had come to Princeton. When Einstein learned what Flexner had done, he was very annoyed and wrote a letter of apology to Eleanor Roosevelt. He and Elsa were then invited to have dinner with the Roosevelts.

The Einsteins liked Princeton and developed a fairly active social life. Elsa told a friend that the town was "one great park with trees."

Trees on the Princeton campus.

Every morning Albert enjoyed walking to his office at the institute. He held occasional seminars, including one on unified field theory even though at the time he was not entirely certain of his work in this area.

He corresponded with Lindemann about plans to spend the summer at Oxford, but by December he decided he did not want to go. According to biographer Ronald Clark, Einstein told a friend that he would "fritter away the summer somewhere in America. Why should an old fellow like me not enjoy relative peace and quiet for once." The peace and quiet of Oxford had always appealed to Einstein. Now, however, he must have recalled the tight security of his last stay in England, and he was reluctant to make himself vulnerable to the Nazis by once again crossing the Atlantic. In March 1934, he informed Lindemann that he did not need his Oxford salary. Perhaps it could be used to aid refugee scholars.

There were other problems involved in returning to Europe. Einstein would have felt obligated to accept invitations he had received to lecture in Madrid and Paris. Also, he and Elsa had relatives in Holland, Belgium, and Switzerland who might have been endangered by Einstein's presence. It was safer for him to remain in America and find a quiet seaside cottage in which to spend the summer. For this happy project, Elsa recruited two of their new friends, Dr. Leon Watters, a wealthy biochemist they had met in Pasadena, and radiologist Dr. Gustav Bucky.

Unfortunately, Elsa did not participate in the vacation. In the late spring of 1934, she received word that her daughter Ilse was extremely ill in Paris. Elsa decided to go back to Europe but left Albert behind because of the Nazis' price on his head. Watters and the Bucky family took Einstein and Helen Dukas to Watch Hill, Rhode Island, where the Buckys had rented a cottage for themselves and the

Einsteins. Watters preferred to stay at a grand old hotel called Ocean House. One night, he invited Einstein and fourteen-year-old Thomas Bucky to have dinner with him. When Watters suggested that they sit in the elegantly furnished lobby, Einstein said he couldn't because he had no socks on.

His eccentricities were remembered long after the one summer he spent in this quiet little resort community. Thomas G. Ahern, who still lives in Watch Hill, recalls seeing Einstein walking on East Beach. "Who could miss him with that wild hair?" says Ahern. "I knew who

The cottage in Watch Hill, where Einstein spent the summer of 1934.

Einstein on vacation.

he was, of course, but I didn't know why he was famous. I was only sixteen." Others couldn't miss Einstein's sailing. Dr. John D. Tobin remembers well the day he and his father went fishing off Watch Hill Lighthouse. At sunset, as they started the outboard motor to head home, they noticed a small sailboat moving in the general direction of Block Island, fourteen miles out to sea. There was no wind at all, and Einstein was riding helplessly on the outgoing tide. Usually he did not mind being becalmed because he could get out his notebook and work on calculations while he waited for the wind to come up. On this occasion, he was grateful to accept a tow. Another time, however, he refused help when the centerboard of the little catboat became stuck firmly in a sandbar at low tide. He waited patiently for high tide to free the boat. There were other hazardous moments, such as when he fetched up on some rocks off Fishers Island, or when he was saved, in the nick of time, from crashing the boat into a sea wall.

The consensus was that Einstein was not a good sailor. He could not name the parts of a sailboat, did not understand the meanings of aids to navigation, could not plot a course with chart and compass, did not bother with life jackets, and could not swim. People in the village learned to look out for him. One day he asked a local character, Louis Dussault, driver of the unofficial town taxi, to take him to the bank. When they pulled up at the Washington Trust Company, Einstein asked the driver to accompany him inside.

"Why would I want to do that?" growled Louis. "It's none of my business what you do in the bank."

"I have to cash a check," Einstein explained patiently. "I need you to identify me because, in this town, no one knows who I am."

Meanwhile, in Paris, Ilse was not doing well. In addition to the French doctors who had been attending her daughter for months, Elsa called in specialists from Germany, but it was too late. In July, Ilse died of cancer. It was a devastating experience for Elsa, and she never completely recovered from her grief. Her surviving daughter, Margot, accompanied her back to the United States and then to Watch Hill for the end of the summer. When Albert and Elsa returned to their Princeton home in the fall, she set up a room as a shrine to Ilse. It included a death mask that Elsa had had cast from her daughter's face, but Einstein insisted she remove the object because it seemed to be a special source of pain.

In the summer of 1935, Elsa herself became ill. A New York specialist diagnosed the swelling in one of her eyes as a symptom of a serious condition in her heart and kidneys. By spring 1936, she seemed a bit better. She and Albert decided to spend a quiet summer at Saranac Lake in the Adirondack Mountains of upstate New York. Bedridden, nursed by her daughter Margot, Elsa wrote a letter to Leon Watters saying that Albert was concentrating on his work so hard that he had no time for her. Despite her comment to Watters, Elsa had tried to encourage Albert to think that her illness was not too serious and that she would soon recover. Einstein, however, may have understood more than she realized. He buried himself in his work to take his mind off his concern for his wife. In a letter to her friend Antonina Vallentin, Elsa noted, "He himself believes his latest work to be the best he has ever done." She also described Einstein as being very sad about her illness. She said she had not realized he loved her so much. When they returned to Princeton in the fall, Elsa's health grew steadily worse. As winter approached, Albert sat by her bed reading to her, and in December she died.

Some people have said that Einstein seemed a bit indifferent to Elsa's death. Others claim that he always kept his feelings to himself and only those very close to him could know how he suffered. It is possible that his love for humanity in general did not carry over to individuals, even his wife. If, in fact, he did keep his feelings to himself, it would be impossible to know his true reaction to Elsa's death. What is known is that he went on working feverishly to bring the principles of quantum mechanics together with relativity in a unified field theory. Since almost no one else was working in this area at the time, it must have been a lonely business.

The problem that interested a great many physicists in the late

*Albert and Elsa just
before her final illness.*

1930s was the splitting of an atomic nucleus to release energy. Laboratory experiments in nuclear fission were being carried out by several scientists, including Enrico Fermi in Italy and Marie Curie's son-in-law, Frédéric Joliot-Curie, in France. In Germany, research in nuclear fission had been carried on by a team made up of Otto Hahn, Fritz Strassman, and Planck's former student Lise Meitner.

Because she was Jewish, Meitner left Germany in 1938 and went to teach at the University of Stockholm in Sweden. Hahn sent her a copy of the final results of their work, and she discussed it with her nephew, who was visiting from Denmark, where he worked in Niels Bohr's laboratory. She concluded that, in splitting a nucleus of uranium, the

Danish physicist Niels Bohr, who in 1938 brought word to Washington, D.C., that a team of German scientists had split an atom of uranium, thereby creating the theoretical knowledge needed to make an atomic bomb.

experiment had released ten times the energy of any previous nuclear reaction. Meitner and her nephew immediately telephoned Bohr in Copenhagen. He then carried the awesome news to the United States and announced it at a conference on theoretical physics in Washington, D.C., in January 1939.

The newly discovered phenomenon had military possibilities. The British government began research and development, but Hahn and other German scientists did not rush to share their knowledge with the Nazi government. Hitler remained poorly informed and only vaguely interested in the atomic research being carried on by German physicists. Scientists outside Germany did not know this and assumed that the Nazis were working feverishly to develop an atomic bomb as a feature of the rearming of Germany.

Leo Szilard, who had emigrated to the United States, was concerned about the possible threat. The largest source of good-quality uranium in the world was in the African nation once called Zaire, now known as the Democratic Republic of Congo. This territory was then ruled by Belgium, and Szilard figured that if Hitler invaded Belgium the Nazis would control most of the uranium in the world. He felt that the Belgian and U.S. governments should be informed of the danger as soon as possible. Believing that he was not well known enough for either government to pay any attention to him, he decided to ask Einstein for help.

In July 1939, Szilard and a colleague tracked Einstein down in Peconic, Long Island, where he was spending his summer vacation at

Physicist Leo Szilard, who drafted a letter to President Roosevelt about the potential dangers of atomic power. Einstein signed the letter.

the cottage of some friends. Einstein was astonished when Szilard explained the situation. Because the field he was working in had almost nothing to do with atomic physics, he had never imagined that, within his lifetime, nuclear fission could actually be used to create a superbomb. He knew it was possible in theory, but he believed that the concept required many more decades of laboratory experiments before it could be a military reality. In his horror that the Nazis might make a bomb soon, Einstein was persuaded to dictate a letter to the Belgian ambassador to the United States. It would be sent first, with a cover note, to the U.S. Department of State. Then Szilard happened to talk with an acquaintance of President Roosevelt, who suggested that the problem could be more quickly brought to governmental attention by a letter directly to Roosevelt himself.

The letter ultimately sent to the White House explained that uranium had been found to be useful in constructing "extremely powerful bombs. . . . A single bomb of this type . . . exploded in a port might very well destroy the whole port." On the subject of uranium, the letter stated that the United States had only small amounts of poor quality uranium ore. "There is some good ore in Canada and the former Czechoslovakia while the most important source is the Belgian Congo. . . . I understand that Germany has actually stopped the sale of uranium from Czechoslovakian mines which she has taken over."

On September 1, 1939, Germany's blitzkrieg, or lightning war, waged by its air force and tank divisions, swept into Poland. England and France then declared war on Germany, and Roosevelt was too preoccupied with the emergency to read a letter from Einstein. He was electrified when he finally did read it and immediately appointed a small group of experts to study the problem. It was chaired by Dr. Lyman Briggs, head of the United States Bureau of Standards. In addition to military representatives, it included such scientists as Leo Szilard, Caltech physicist J. Robert Oppenheimer, and Enrico Fermi, then at Columbia University. Fermi had been awarded the 1938 Nobel Prize in physics, and instead of going back to Italy after receiving the prize in Stockholm, he and his Jewish wife had fled to the United States.

Right: American physicist J. Robert Oppenheimer, one of the scientists who helped develop the first atomic bomb.

Below: Italian physicist Enrico Fermi, who immigrated to the United States and worked on the bomb, shown here years after World War II.

Einstein was also invited to be a member of the Briggs committee but politely refused. If he had accepted, he might have been prevented from joining. Ever since his arrival in the United States he had been under investigation by the FBI because of his pacifist and radical views. Einstein was suspected of being a Communist and therefore considered a security risk. FBI director J. Edgar Hoover would continue the investigation for the rest of Einstein's life. Unaware of FBI activity, Einstein probably declined because he felt that by sending the letter he had already compromised his pacifist principles enough. But as events unfolded in Europe, he continued to have the painfully mixed feelings about pacifism that he had been experiencing since 1933.

In 1940, Hitler invaded Belgium. He also took Denmark, Norway, and the Netherlands. The German blitzkrieg pushed the British army back to Dunkirk on the English Channel, where the evacuation of the troops in small boats was heroic. France surrendered to Germany. While Britain fought on alone, Szilard and Fermi were given secret funds to conduct atomic research at Columbia University. That year, Einstein became an American citizen.

On December 7, 1941, the Japanese bombed U.S. installations at Pearl Harbor. Since Japan had an alliance with Germany, the United States declared war on both countries, and World War II became truly global. Just after the Japanese attack, Einstein was asked to solve some theoretical problems connected with the use of uranium for nuclear weapons. The work was brought to him at Princeton, and in a few days he produced the necessary answers. It was one piece in a large puzzle, and although Einstein must have guessed something of its purpose, he was not officially informed about how his work would fit into nuclear research. He was happy to do what he could for his new country and later was a part-time consultant for the navy. The

Above: Helen Dukas, Einstein, and his step-daughter Margot are sworn in as U.S. citizens, 1940.

Right: U.S. President Franklin D. Roosevelt signs the declaration of war on Japan after that nation bombed Pearl Harbor.

FBI investigation of his background, however, meant that officials did not want to trust him with the big picture.

The letter to Roosevelt and his work on a set of problems concerning the use of uranium were as close as Einstein ever came to being directly involved in the creation of the bomb. The Briggs committee evolved into the Manhattan Project, which was established at the testing grounds at Los Alamos, New Mexico, in 1942. By this time, Einstein's health had become fragile, and he had to confine himself to Princeton. Scientists worked on aspects of the project in separate groups, and they were not allowed to learn what the other groups were doing. They were also forbidden to discuss the project with scientists outside of Los Alamos. A radio broadcast gave Einstein his first knowledge of the bomb that was dropped on the Japanese port of Hiroshima on August 6, 1945, killing seventy thousand people instantly. He was stunned.

Four months earlier, Einstein had officially retired from the institute, but by special arrangement he kept his office and continued to work there two or three days a week. Eventually, having regretted signing the letter to Roosevelt, he returned to pacifist work as the head of a committee to educate the public about the horror and immorality of atomic weapons. Russia and its wartime allies had drifted apart, beginning an era of distrust that came to be called the cold war. Einstein had an overwhelming fear that the situation would degenerate into an atomic war destroying at least two-thirds of the world's population.

As well as having fears about the future, Einstein had to live with grim stories of the recent past. For example, his friend and fellow professor Abraham Pais at the institute told Einstein of his time in a Nazi prison. He and a colleague had been arrested for being involved in a

The second atomic bomb is dropped on the Japanese city of Nagasaki.

plan to care for orphans of Jewish parents lost in the concentration camps. The colleague was executed for having a letter about the plan in his pocket. Pais was released. He told Einstein that he could just as easily have been the one to carry the letter in his pocket. Einstein himself had scars in his memory that intensified his support of Zionism. In 1944, he learned of a tragic catastrophe that had befallen the family of his cousin Roberto Einstein, son of his uncle Jakob. Nazi soldiers had murdered Roberto's wife and two daughters and burned down their house in a village near Florence, Italy. In addition, several of Einstein's cousins had died in the concentration camps of Theresienstadt and Auschwitz.

Einstein makes a broadcast about the immorality of war.

The end of World War II in 1945 fully revealed the vast horror of the Holocaust, during which six million Jews and other innocent victims perished in Nazi concentration camps. This colossal mass atrocity and the rise of Nazism that led to it might have offered a grim lesson for the future. By 1950, however, many Americans seemed hypnotized by a national hysteria resembling the fever of Nazism that overwhelmed Germany in the 1930s. Escalating tensions with Joseph Stalin's Soviet Union were creating a nationwide fear that Communists were trying to take over the United States.

Einstein must have been reminded of the Germany he left behind in 1933. He was especially alarmed when he learned the fate of some lawyers who had defended American Communist Party members accused of conspiring to overthrow the government. The trial itself was an acceptable legal process, but afterward the lawyers who had represented the accused Communists were sentenced to jail for contempt of court. Disrespect for the court may have been part of the lawyers' strategy, but a number of people, including Einstein, protested that jailing them was unconstitutional. The Sixth Amendment to the Constitution of the United States guarantees every person accused of a crime the right to a "public trial . . . and to have the assistance of counsel for his defense." The protest inspired FBI director J. Edgar Hoover to intensify his secret investigation. In one report he linked Einstein with dozens of Communist-front organizations. "He is principally a pacifist and could be considered a liberal thinker," wrote Hoover.

Meanwhile, in Wheeling, West Virginia, Senator Joseph McCarthy of Wisconsin had given a speech claiming he had clear evidence that the U.S. Department of State was full of Communist spies. A Senate investigation cleared the State Department and proved that the charges were false. Nevertheless, McCarthy repeated his accusations on radio and television and refused to produce hard evidence when challenged. Reelected in 1952, the senator continued his flagrantly hateful campaign against alleged Communists and subversives, ultimately destroying the careers of many innocent people.

Newspaper columnists and radio commentators picked up new rumors and fanned the flames of hysteria that eventually scorched Einstein. He began receiving hate mail, and a surprising number of cranks managed to find the way to Mercer Street in Princeton. Helen Dukas had to establish a strategy with the neighbors. Whenever someone called, Dukas opened the front door, but Einstein would stand behind the locked screen door. After the crank delivered his poisonous and hateful remarks, one neighbor or another would come over and say soothing things to the crank and then escort him away. With such a barrage of hatred in the media, in the mail, and even at his doorstep, it is a wonder Einstein did not take the chance to leave the country when it was offered.

In 1948, Einstein's old Zionist friend, Chaim Weizmann, had become the first president of the new state of Israel. It was primarily an honorary office, and when he died in 1952 several people suggested that Einstein should be appointed the next president. Israel's elected leader, Prime Minister David Ben Gurion, said, "Why not have the most illustrious Jew in the world, and possibly the greatest man alive—Einstein?" He then asked Abba Eban, Israel's ambassador to the United States, to telephone Einstein and sound him out on his probable reaction to an invitation to be president.

Politely, Einstein explained that although he knew "a little about nature," he really did not know enough about people to qualify for the job. Ben Gurion refused to accept this preliminary refusal and

Prime Minister David Ben Gurion, who asked Einstein to become president of Israel after the death of Chaim Weizmann.

insisted that the public duties connected to the office would not prevent Einstein from carrying on his scientific work. A formal invitation was offered, to which Einstein replied that although he was "deeply moved" he was unable to accept the honor. "I lack both the natural aptitude and the experience to deal properly with people and to exercise official functions," he wrote. "For these reasons alone I should be unsuited to fulfill the duties of that high office, even if advancing age was not making increasing inroads on my strength."

Einstein's strength had indeed been waning. Since 1948, he had been living with an aneurysm, or ballooning, in the wall of his abdominal aorta, the main internal artery. The doctor who had discovered it said that it was too late for surgery. Quite likely it would burst someday and kill him. Margot, who had earlier looked after her mother and then Einstein's stroke-ridden sister, Maja, until her death in 1951, now took care of her stepfather.

By December 1954, he was virtually an invalid. Abraham Pais went to see him at his home and found him sitting in his study, his legs covered with a blanket, looking at a pad of paper on his lap. "He was working," wrote Pais. "He put his pad aside at once and greeted me. We spent a pleasant half hour or so. . . . I said good-bye. I walked to the door of the study. . . . I turned around as I opened the door. I saw him in his chair, his pad back on his lap, a pencil in his hand, oblivious to his surroundings. He was back at work."

In March 1955, Einstein learned that his old friend Michele Besso had died of a stroke. "What I most admired about him," he wrote to Besso's family, "is that he managed to live for many years not only in peace but also in lasting harmony with a woman—an undertaking in which I have twice failed rather disgracefully." Besso had died the day after Einstein's seventy-sixth birthday.

Einstein making notes in his Princeton study. This is how his friend and colleague Abraham Pais last saw him.

A month later, Einstein himself collapsed at home and after being nursed for a few days, he was taken to the hospital. The aneurysm had burst, and he refused emergency surgery to patch his aorta, explaining that he did not believe in "artificially prolonging life." Three doctors tried, unsuccessfully, to persuade him to change his mind and submit to a new surgical technique. So did Dr. Gustav Bucky and Thomas Bucky, now also a doctor. Hans Albert, who had flown from California, said he would try again the next day, but at 1:15 A.M. Albert Einstein died in his sleep. "He faced death humbly and quietly," Margot wrote later. "He left the world without sentimentality or regrets."

Pais once said that Einstein's laugh was a wonderful bark "like a contented seal." That laughter would certainly have been heard in Princeton if its owner could have seen the swarm of newspaper reporters and television crews that poured into Mercer Street on the morning of April 18, 1955. Einstein had insisted that it would be absurd to make the house into a shrine. His will called for cremation with his ashes to be scattered in a river so there could be no pilgrimages to a burial site, and his brain was to be preserved for scientific study. An autopsy revealed that surgery on the aorta would have been futile.

It seems a fitting memorial that his work continues. In the 1930s, 1940s, and into the 1950s, Einstein was probably the only physicist in the world searching for a bridge between relativity and quantum physics, a unified theory to explain all the forces of nature. None of his thinking could be verified in laboratory experiments at the time, and many scientists dismissed the work as useless. Michael White and John Gribbin, coauthors of a recent biography of Einstein, write that now his lonely work is "one of the most fruitful areas of research for physicists seeking a theory of everything." Dr. Stephen Hawking, the well-known English physicist at Cambridge University, hopes that a unified field theory will be found some time in the first years of the twenty-first century.

But when the theory is proven, we still will not know all that there is to know about the universe. As Einstein once said, "I live and I feel puzzled, and all the time I try to understand."

$$\sum \frac{1}{\sqrt{1-u^2}} = \sum \frac{1}{\sqrt{1-\bar{u}^2}} \qquad \mathcal{E} = \mathcal{E}_0' + m\left(\frac{1}{\sqrt{1-u^2}} - 1\right)$$

$$\sum \frac{u_i}{\sqrt{1-u^2}} = \sum \frac{\bar{u}_i}{\sqrt{1-\bar{u}^2}}$$

Ein. L. K': $\quad 2\mathcal{E}_0 + 2m\left(\frac{1}{\sqrt{1-u'^2}} - 1\right) = 2\overline{\mathcal{E}_0} + 2\bar{u}$

Ein. L. K: $\quad 2\mathcal{E}_0 + m\left(\frac{1}{\sqrt{1-u^2}} - 1\right) + m\left(\frac{1}{\sqrt{1-u^2}} - 1\right) = 2\overline{\mathcal{E}_0}$

$$\mathcal{E}_0 - m + \frac{m}{\sqrt{1-u'^2}\sqrt{1-v^2}} = \overline{\mathcal{E}_0} - \bar{m} + \frac{m}{\sqrt{1-\bar{u}'^2}\sqrt{1-v}}$$

$$\mathcal{E}_0 - m + \frac{m}{\sqrt{1-u'^2}} = \overline{\mathcal{E}_0} - \bar{m} + \frac{\bar{m}}{\sqrt{1-\bar{u}'^2}}$$

$$\left[\left(\overline{\mathcal{E}_0} - \mathcal{E}_0\right) - \left(\bar{m} - m\right)\right]\left(\frac{1}{\sqrt{1-v^2}} - 1\right) =$$

$$\neq 0$$

CHRONOLOGY

1879 Albert Einstein is born in Ulm, Germany, on March 14.

1880 The Einstein family moves to Munich.

1881 Albert's sister, Maria, called Maja, is born on November 18.

1886 Albert begins elementary school at a Catholic public school.

1888 Albert enters Luitpold Gymnasium; courses include Judaism.

1889 Max Talmey introduces Albert to numerous books on science.

1894 Einsteins move to Milan, leaving Albert in Munich to finish school.

1895 Albert leaves school without finishing and goes to his family in Italy. Fails entrance exam for the Zurich technical institute, Eidgenossische Technische Hochschule (ETH). Enrolls in high school at Aarau, Switzerland.

1896 Albert finishes high school and enrolls at ETH. Meets future wife, classmate Mileva Maric.

1899 Albert applies for Swiss citizenship.

1900 Albert graduates from ETH but cannot find a job.

1901 Einstein is granted Swiss citizenship. He takes a temporary teaching job at Winterthur and then another in Schaffhausen.

1902 Einstein moves to Bern, offers tutoring in math and physics. Liserl, Albert and Mileva's daughter, is born at Mileva's parents' home in Serbia. Einstein and two friends form discussion group, later called the Olympia Academy. Einstein takes a job with the Swiss patent office. His father, Hermann, dies in Milan.

1903 Mileva Maric and Albert Einstein are married on January 6.

1904 Hans Albert, Mileva and Albert's first son, is born on May 14.

1905 *Annalen der Physik* publishes four scientific papers by Einstein, one of them about the special theory of relativity.

1908 University of Bern accepts Einstein as *privatdozent,* or apprentice lecturer.

1909 An honorary doctorate is awarded to Einstein by the University of Geneva. Among the other honorees are Ernest Solvay of Belgium and Marie Curie of France. Einstein resigns from the University of Bern to accept a position as associate professor at the University of Zurich.

1910 Eduard, Mileva and Albert's second son, is born on July 28.

1911 Einstein accepts a position as full professor at the University of Prague, then in the Austrian Empire, now the capital of the Czech Republic. He goes to Brussels for the first Solvay Congress, a gathering of leading European scientists presided over by the Dutch physicist Hendrick Lorentz.

1912 ETH offers a professorship, and the Einsteins move back to Zurich. Grossmann helps Einstein work out the mathematical basis for the general theory of relativity, which includes Einstein's prediction of the effect of gravity on light.

1913 Max Planck and Walther Nernst come to Zurich to persuade Einstein to work in Berlin. Einstein eventually accepts three positions: professor at the University of Berlin, member of the Prussian Academy of Sciences, and director of the Kaiser Wilhelm Gesellschaft.

1914 The Einstein family moves to Berlin. In the summer, Mileva takes the two boys back to Zurich. World War I breaks out.

1915 Einstein signs the "Manifesto for Europeans" as a protest against German militarism. He completes the final structure of the general theory of relativity.

1916 *Annalen der Physik* publishes Einstein's paper on the general theory of relativity. He writes papers on quantum physics and first begins to doubt the element of uncertainty in the theory.

1917 Intense work schedule and wartime food shortages cause Einstein to collapse with a stomach ulcer, jaundice, and severe depression. Ill for more than a year, he is nursed by his cousin Elsa Lowenthal, a divorcée living in Berlin with her two teenage daughters, Margot and Ilse.

1918 In Zurich to visit sons, Albert asks Mileva for a divorce. World War I ends November 11.

1919 Mileva and Einstein are divorced in February. In May, two British expeditions organized by Arthur Eddington photograph an eclipse of the sun in Brazil and West Africa to prove Einstein's prediction of the effect of gravity on light. In June, Albert and Elsa are married. In November, the results of the Eddington expeditions are announced in London. Overnight, the news media make Einstein into an international celebrity.

1920 Pauline, Einstein's mother, dies of cancer. Anti-Semitism begins to become aggressive in Berlin, and Einstein is booed at some of his lectures. He attempts to develop a low profile by lecturing in universities outside of Germany and meets Danish physicist Niels Bohr for the first time.

1921 Chaim Weizmann invites Einstein to join in a trip to the United States to raise money for the Jewish National Fund and particularly for the founding of Hebrew University in Jerusalem. The Einsteins and the Weizmanns are paraded through New York. They visit Boston, Chicago, Washington D.C., and Princeton. Back in Berlin Einstein meets a Hungarian physics student named Leo Szilard.

1922 Walther Rathenau, German foreign minister, is assassinated in Berlin because he is a Jew. Elsa and Albert travel by ship to Japan, where Einstein gives lectures. Returning by sea, they learn he has been awarded the 1921 Nobel Prize in physics.

1923 The Einsteins visit the future site of Hebrew University in Jerusalem and return to Berlin via Spain and France. Einstein visits sons in Zurich and notes Eduard's mental problems. He publishes two articles about his work toward a unified field theory, a common basis for relativity and quantum theory. Uncontrollable inflation sweeps Germany and Hitler makes a grab for political power.

1924 Working in Berlin, Einstein learns of the work of Satyenda Bose in India and Louis de Broglie in France on the physics of light. He credits them in his paper on the wave-particle nature of light.

1927 Elsa and Albert call on Sigmund Freud when he visits Berlin.

1928 Friend and mentor Hendrick Lorentz dies, and Einstein speaks at his funeral. He collapses after a lecture in Davos, Switzerland. During his long recuperation, Elsa hires Helen Dukas, who becomes Einstein's lifelong secretary.

1929 Einstein retreats to a country cottage to avoid fiftieth birthday celebration. City council of Berlin attempts to honor him with the gift of a country home, but the effort is stymied several times. Albert and Elsa spend their own money to build a cottage at Caputh on the Havel River. Due in part to a worldwide financial crash, the Nazi party begins to gather wide support.

1930 The Einsteins visit the United States to spend the winter at the California Institute of Technology in Pasadena.

1931 Elsa and Albert return for another winter at Caltech. They visit Oxford, and he receives a research fellowship at Christ Church College.

1932   Einstein is appointed to a professorship at the new Institute for Advanced Study in Princeton with the understanding that he will divide his time between there and Berlin.

1933   The Einsteins spend another winter at Caltech. Hitler comes to power in Germany. While sailing home, the Einsteins learn that their house in Caputh has been searched by Nazi police, their Berlin apartment raided, and their bank account impounded. They stop in Belgium temporarily. Einstein makes visits to Switzerland and England. In October, the Einsteins and Dukas sail to the United States, where they settle in Princeton.

1934   Elsa goes to Paris, where her daughter Ilse is dying. After the death, daughter Margot brings her mother back to the United States.

1936   Elsa Einstein dies in December.

1939   Einstein's sister, Maja, comes to live in Princeton. World War II begins in Europe. Einstein signs a letter drafted by Szilard to President Roosevelt discussing the locations of worldwide uranium resources and expressing concern that the Germans may be making an atomic bomb.

1940   Einstein becomes a U.S. citizen.

1941   The Japanese bomb Pearl Harbor and the United States joins the war.

1943   Einstein becomes a consultant to the U.S. Navy.

1945   An American plane drops an atomic bomb on the Japanese port of Hiroshima, killing seventy thousand people. World War II ends.

1946 Einstein renews his commitment to pacifism, heading a committee to educate the public about the immorality of war.

1948 Doctors discover an aortic aneurysm in Einstein's abdomen. He is informed that if it bursts it will be fatal.

1950 Einstein and others protest the jailing of lawyers who defended American Communists in a conspiracy trial. This causes FBI director J. Edgar Hoover to step up his secret investigation of Einstein. Senator Joseph McCarthy of Wisconsin begins his four-year anti-Communist campaign.

1951 Maja dies at home in Princeton.

1952 Rumors that Einstein is a subversive bring hateful cranks to Einstein's door in Princeton. Einstein is invited to become president of Israel but refuses.

1954 Einstein's fragile health prevents him from leaving his house.

1955 In April, Einstein collapses at home and is taken to Princeton Hospital. He refuses surgery on his ruptured aortic aneurysm and dies in his sleep at 1:15 A.M., April 18.

BIBLIOGRAPHY

Brian, Denis. *Einstein: A Life*. New York: John Wiley & Sons, 1996.

Calaprice, Alice, ed. *The Quotable Einstein*. Princeton, New Jersey: Princeton University Press, 1996.

Calder, Nigel. *Einstein's Universe*. London: Penguin Books Ltd., 1990.

Clark, Ronald W. *Einstein: The Life and Times*. New York: World Publishing, 1971.

Coleman, James A. *Relativity for the Layman*. New York: Signet, New American Library, 1958.

Davies, Paul. *About Time: Einstein's Unfinished Revolution*. New York: Simon & Schuster, 1995.

Dukas, Helen, and Banesh Hoffman, eds. *Albert Einstein: The Human Side, New Glimpses from His Archives*. Princeton, New Jersey: Princeton University Press, 1979.

Einstein, Albert. *Out of My Later Years*. New York: Philosophical Library, 1950.

_____. *The World As I See It*. Secaucus, New Jersey: Carol Publishing Group, 1997.

Feynman, Richard P. *Six Not-So-Easy Pieces: Einstein's Relativity, Symmetry, and Space-Time*. Reading, Massachusetts: Addison-Wesley, 1963.

Frank, Philipp. *Einstein: His Life and Times*. New York: Da Capo, 1953.

Gamow, George. *Gravity*. Garden City, New York: Doubleday, Anchor Books, 1962.

_____. *The Great Physicists from Galileo to Einstein*. New York: Dover Publications, Inc. 1988.

_____. *Mr Tompkins in Paperback*. Cambridge, England: Cambridge University Press, 1993.

_____. *Thirty Years That Shook Physics*. New York: Dover Publications, Inc. 1985.

Geroch, Robert. *General Relativity from A to B*. Chicago: University of Chicago Press, 1981.

Gibilisco, Stan. *Understanding Einstein's Theories of Relativity: Man's New Perspective on the Cosmos*. New York: Dover Publications, Inc. 1983

Heisenberg, Werner. *Encounters with Einstein*. Princeton, New Jersey: Princeton University Press, 1983.

Hey, Tony, and Patrick Walters. *Einstein's Mirror.* Cambridge, England: Cambridge University Press, 1997.

Highfield, Roger, and Paul Carter. *The Private Lives of Albert Einstein.* New York: St. Martin's Press, 1993.

Lightman, Alan. *Einstein's Dreams.* New York: Warner Books, 1993.

Pais, Abraham. *'Subtle Is the Lord . . .' The Science and the Life of Albert Einstein.* New York: Oxford University Press, 1982.

Vallentin, Antonina. *The Drama of Albert Einstein.* Translated by Moura Budberg. Garden City, New York: Doubleday, 1954.

White, Michael, and John Gribbin. *Einstein: A Life in Science.* New York: Dutton, 1994.

Wolf, Fred Alan. *Taking the Quantum Leap.* New York: Harper & Row, 1989.

Zajonc, Arthur. *Catching the Light: The Entwined History of Light and Mind.* New York: Oxford University Press, 1995.

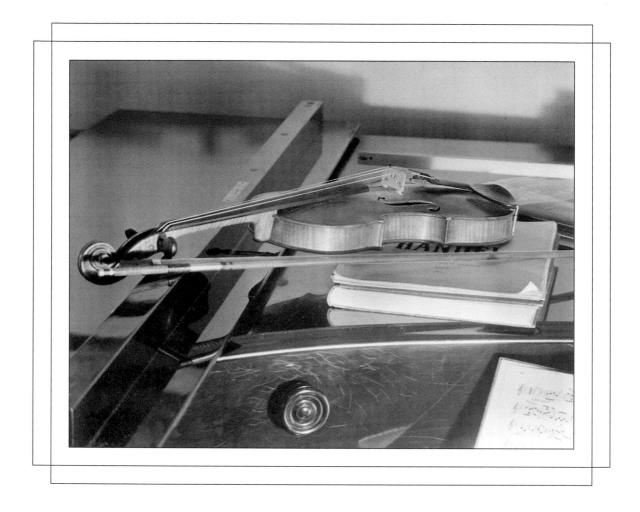

ACKNOWLEDGMENTS

Dorothy Briley, editor-in-chief and publisher of Clarion Books, accepted this project for publication but died before she could see the final manuscript. She was my publishing mentor for three previous books and I shall miss her.

For continuing support and encouragement, I thank Dinah Stevenson, Clarion's new vice president and editorial director, and I truly appreciate the constructive comments and queries offered by my new editor, Virginia Buckley. Without the kindly guidance of John Logan of Princeton, University, I would not have found some unexpected photo sources or the invaluable services of Jack Scott at the University of Maryland and the cordial assistance of Gary Samson at the University of New Hampshire. And, as always, I must thank my wife, Sylvia, for her indefatigable help in photo research and for her superior expertise as a book designer.

John B. Severance

PICTURE CREDITS

Archive Photos: frontispiece, 8, 14, 24, 36, 47, 48 top, 50, 66, 75, 86, 103, 111, 118. Archive Photos/America Stock: 93, 115 top. Archive Photos/Leo Baeck Institute: 25. Archive Photos/Camerique: 11 bottom. Archive Photos/Express Newspapers/A934: 120. Archive Photos/Thomas H. Hartshorne: 31. Archive Photos/Illustrated London News: 80. Archive Photos/Eugene Kone: 110. Archive Photos/London Daily Express: 132. Archive Photos/New York Times: 84. Archive Photos/Irving Newman: 124. Archive Photos/Popperfoto: 52, 62, 65, 109.

Einstein Archives, Hebrew University of Jerusalem: 28, 33, 54, 102.

Gandhi National Museum, New Delhi, India: 70.

Imperial War Museum, London, England: 58, 59, 76, 91.

Library of Congress, Washington, D. C.: 11 top, 13, 18, 22 top left, top right, and bottom, 27, 43, 44, 48 bottom, 57, 72, 96, 113 top and bottom, 115 bottom, 117.

Lotte Jacobi Archives, Photographic Services, University of New Hampshire: 16, 19, 30, 38, 88, 90, 98, 100, 106, 122, 136.

John B. Severance: 105.

INDEX

Page numbers in *italic* type refer to illustrations.